Less Stuff, More Life: The Art of Decluttering for Happiness and Freedom

The Decluttering Method That Works for Everyone

By

(J.R. Mendoza)

COPYRIGHT

This is a work of creative nonfiction. Some parts have been fictionalized in varying degrees for various purposes.

DISCLAIMER

This guide is intended for information and educational purposes only. In no event shall its authors, publishers, suppliers or partners be liable for any damages (including without limitation, damages for loss of data or profit, or due to business interruption) arising out of the use or inability to use the materials in this guide. Readers are advised to conduct their own research and due diligence and consult with a qualified professional before making any purchasing or financial decisions.

DISCLOSURE

This electronic version of this book may include hyperlinks to products and learning resources for reader convenience. The authors participate in various affiliate programs which may cover some of the tools and resources mentioned in this guide. This means they may earn a nominal fee on purchases from related partner websites.

Dedication

This book is especially dedicated to:

To my wife, life partner and infinite strength:

Thank you for being my daily inspiration, for reminding me that what is essential is not found in material things, but in the simplicity of the moments we share and in the love we cultivate together.

To my daughter:

Your laughter and purity have taught me that happiness lies in the simple, and in what really matters. Your way of seeing the world motivated me to reflect on what order really means.

This book is a tribute to the impact you both have had on my life.

Special Thanks

This book is possible thanks to the support of all the team that surrounds me in the agency, I am sure that without you none of this would be possible. Thank you all and I will be eternally grateful for all your efforts.

EMPORIUM DIGITAL ONLINE LTD

83 Ducie Street, Manchester,

Greater Manchester, United Kingdom, M1 2JQ.

About the author

J.R. Mendoza is a professional with a solid background in social communication, advertising and marketing. As a specialist in sales, finance, digital business and social media management, he combines his technical knowledge with a deep interest in personal growth. His multidisciplinary approach makes him an author capable of tackling complex issues with a unique perspective, enriched by years of experience in the corporate and digital world, helping people to reach their full potential.

Table of Contents

Introduction

In our modern world, it's easy to find ourselves surrounded by an overwhelming amount of "stuff." Physical clutter fills our homes, digital clutter clogs our devices, and mental clutter occupies our thoughts, leaving us feeling drained, stressed, and stuck. This book, *Less Stuff, More Life: The Art of Decluttering for Happiness and Freedom,* is not just about tidying up or organizing your belongings—it's about creating space for what truly matters, rediscovering joy, and regaining control over your life.

The Purpose of the Book: Why Decluttering Is Essential for Reducing Stress and Boosting Productivity

At its core, decluttering is more than a simple act of discarding unused items or organizing files—it's a powerful tool for transforming your life. Clutter doesn't just take up physical space; it also occupies mental and emotional bandwidth, leaving little room for creativity, focus, or peace of mind. When your surroundings are chaotic, your thoughts tend to mirror that disarray, creating a perpetual cycle of stress and distraction.

Studies have shown that a cluttered environment can lead to heightened stress levels, reduced productivity, and even strained relationships. The simple act of decluttering, on the other hand, has the potential to significantly improve mental clarity, emotional well-being, and overall life satisfaction.

This book is designed to guide you through the process of shedding excess baggage—whether it's physical, digital, or emotional—to create an environment that supports, rather than hinders, your personal and professional goals. By embracing the principles of decluttering, you'll find yourself better equipped to focus on what truly matters, achieve greater productivity, and experience a sense of freedom that comes with living intentionally.

But decluttering isn't just about reducing stress—it's about making space for joy. Imagine walking into a home that feels like a sanctuary, where every item has a purpose and brings you happiness. Picture sitting down to work at a clean, organized desk, free from distractions, and being able to focus fully on your tasks. By decluttering, you're not just removing what no longer serves you; you're creating space for experiences, opportunities, and relationships that bring fulfillment and purpose.

Who This Book Is for: Identifying Readers Who Seek Freedom from Clutter

This book is for anyone who has ever felt burdened by the weight of clutter in their life. You may be a busy professional struggling to keep your workspace organized, a parent trying to manage the chaos of a household, or someone who feels overwhelmed by the sheer volume of "stuff" in their home. Perhaps you've tried decluttering before but found it difficult to maintain the results or didn't know where to start. Wherever you are on your journey, this book is here to help.

If you've ever found yourself saying things like, "I just don't have enough time," "I can't focus with all this mess," or "I don't even know where to begin," then this book is for you. It's for the person who feels stuck in a cycle of accumulation and distraction and wants to reclaim control over their surroundings and their life.

This book is also for those who struggle with digital and mental clutter. In today's world, where we're constantly bombarded with notifications, emails, and endless streams of information, it's easy to feel mentally overloaded. The principles outlined in this book will not only help you declutter your physical spaces but also provide tools for managing digital chaos and achieving mental clarity.

Finally, this book is for anyone seeking a more intentional, minimalist lifestyle. If you're ready to embrace the philosophy of "less is more" and focus on what truly matters, you'll find this guide to be a valuable resource.

What to Expect: A Transformative Journey from Overwhelm to Peace

Decluttering is often seen as a daunting task, but it doesn't have to be. This book is designed to break the process down into manageable steps, making it accessible and achievable for everyone, regardless of your starting point.

You can expect a practical, hands-on approach to decluttering that goes beyond surface-level tidying. Each chapter focuses on a specific aspect of clutter—whether it's physical, digital, or mental—and provides actionable strategies for tackling it effectively.

Here's a glimpse of the journey ahead:

- Understanding the Impact of Clutter: You'll learn how clutter affects your mental health, productivity, and overall well-being. By identifying the hidden costs of clutter, you'll gain a deeper appreciation for why it's essential to declutter.

- Assessing Your Starting Point: Before diving into the decluttering process, you'll take stock of your current situation, identify pain points, and track patterns contributing to clutter. This step lays the foundation for meaningful change.

- Shifting Your Mindset: Decluttering isn't just about the physical act of discarding items—it's about changing the way you think about possessions, perfectionism, and emotional attachments. This book will help you adopt a mindset that supports long-term success.

- Setting Clear Goals and Priorities: You'll define what a clutter-free life looks like for you, set realistic goals, and prioritize areas that will have the greatest impact on your well-being.

- Building Your Toolkit: From essential supplies to digital tools and support systems, you'll gather everything you need to embark on your decluttering journey with confidence.

- Developing a Strategy: With a clear plan in place, you'll tackle clutter systematically using proven methods like the 5-step decluttering process and the Four-Box Method.

- Decluttering Specific Spaces: This book provides room-by-room guidance for decluttering your home, as well as tips for organizing your workplace and managing digital clutter.

- Maintaining a Clutter-Free Life: The journey doesn't end once you've decluttered—it's about creating habits and systems to ensure lasting results. You'll learn how to prevent clutter from creeping back in and embrace a philosophy of intentional living.

- Reaping the Benefits: Finally, you'll explore the profound impact of decluttering on your life, from reducing stress and boosting productivity to creating a sense of peace and purpose.

By the end of this book, you'll have the tools, mindset, and motivation to transform your life through the art of decluttering. But more importantly, you'll have the freedom to focus on what truly matters—whether it's spending time with loved ones, pursuing your passions, or simply enjoying the calm of a clutter-free environment.

Decluttering is not just about the physical act of organizing; it's a lifestyle shift that allows you to live with intention, purpose, and joy. As you embark on this journey, remember that it's not about achieving perfection but about creating a life that feels meaningful and fulfilling.

So, take a deep breath, clear some space, and let's get started. A life of happiness, freedom, and clarity awaits!

Chapter 1: Understanding the Impact of Clutter

What Is Clutter? Exploring Physical, Digital, and Mental Clutter

Clutter is more than just a pile of unused items or a messy desk—it's a state of disarray that can invade every aspect of our lives. Clutter doesn't discriminate between physical spaces, digital platforms, or the mind; it infiltrates them all, often without us even realizing the extent of its impact. To effectively tackle clutter, it's important to first understand its different forms and how each type affects our overall well-being.

1. Physical Clutter

Physical clutter is what most people think of when they hear the word "clutter." It's the visible accumulation of objects that no longer serve a purpose or bring joy. This can include everything from old clothes and unused gadgets to piles of paper and overflowing drawers.

Common Sources of Physical Clutter

- Accumulated Possessions: Items we no longer need but keep out of habit or guilt, such as clothes that no longer fit or gifts we feel obligated to keep.
- Procrastination: Delaying decisions about what to do with items, such as junk mail that's tossed on the counter or boxes left unpacked for years.
- Sentimental Attachments: Holding onto things for their emotional value, like childhood mementos or family heirlooms, even when they take up unnecessary space.
- Excessive Consumerism: Constantly buying new items without clearing out old ones, leading to overcrowded spaces.

The Impact of Physical Clutter

Physical clutter can be overwhelming, making your home or workspace feel chaotic and stressful. Studies have shown that living in a cluttered environment can raise cortisol levels, the hormone associated with stress. A cluttered home may also contribute to feelings of guilt, frustration, or shame, especially if you feel embarrassed to invite others into your space.

Clutter not only impacts your mental state but also reduces productivity. Imagine trying to work at a desk covered in papers, books, and random objects. The time spent searching for what you need adds up, draining your energy and focus.

Recognizing Physical Clutter

To identify physical clutter, ask yourself:

- Does this item serve a functional purpose or bring me joy?
- When was the last time I used this?
- If I didn't have it, would I buy it again?

If the answer to these questions is "no," then it's likely time to part with the item.

2. Digital Clutter

Digital clutter is the modern-day equivalent of a messy attic. Unlike physical clutter, it's not always visible, but its effects are just as disruptive. Digital clutter includes everything from unread emails and disorganized files to unused apps and excessive notifications.

Common Sources of Digital Clutter

- Email Overload: Hundreds or even thousands of unread messages, many of which are irrelevant or outdated.
- Unorganized Files: Randomly named files scattered across your desktop, making it difficult to find what you need.
- Unused Apps and Programs: Applications downloaded but rarely, if ever, used, taking up valuable storage space.
- Excessive Subscriptions: Notifications, newsletters, and updates that clog your inbox and distract you from what's important.
- Social Media Chaos: Following too many accounts, consuming irrelevant content, or feeling overwhelmed by endless scrolling.

The Impact of Digital Clutter

Digital clutter can feel less tangible than physical clutter, but its consequences are very real. A cluttered inbox or desktop can lead to decision fatigue, making even small tasks feel overwhelming. Constant notifications and the pressure to keep up with digital demands can increase stress and reduce focus.

Furthermore, digital clutter often creates inefficiencies. For instance, wasting time searching for a document you know you saved somewhere can hinder productivity. Additionally, excessive digital clutter can make it difficult to disconnect from technology, contributing to poor work-life balance and mental fatigue.

Recognizing Digital Clutter

Signs of digital clutter include:

- Regularly feeling overwhelmed by your email inbox.
- Struggling to locate important files or documents.
- Not using or forgetting about apps or subscriptions you've paid for.
- Spending too much time managing notifications or scrolling aimlessly.

To combat digital clutter, begin by assessing your digital habits and identifying areas that create unnecessary stress or distraction.

3. Mental Clutter

Mental clutter is perhaps the most invisible yet impactful type of clutter. It refers to the constant stream of thoughts, worries, and to-do lists that occupy your mind. This can stem from an overwhelming schedule, unresolved emotions, or a lack of boundaries.

Common Sources of Mental Clutter

- Over commitment: Taking on too many responsibilities and struggling to manage them all.
- Unfinished Tasks: A running list of things you know you need to do but haven't addressed yet.
- Worry and Anxiety: Stressing about the future, replaying past mistakes, or obsessing over things beyond your control.
- Information Overload: Consuming excessive news, social media, or other content, leading to a sense of overwhelm.
- Perfectionism: Holding yourself to unrealistic standards, which can lead to paralysis and self-doubt.

The Impact of Mental Clutter

Mental clutter affects your ability to focus, make decisions, and enjoy the present moment. It can lead to feelings of stress, burnout, and even depression. When your mind is constantly preoccupied, it's difficult to be fully present in your relationships, work, or personal life.

Moreover, mental clutter often spills into other areas, making it harder to tackle physical or digital clutter. For example, feeling mentally overwhelmed might cause you to procrastinate on organizing your home or managing your inbox, perpetuating a cycle of disarray.

Recognizing Mental Clutter

Signs of mental clutter include:

- Frequently feeling overwhelmed or unable to concentrate.
- Struggling to sleep due to racing thoughts.
- Difficulty prioritizing tasks or making decisions.
- Feeling constantly "busy" without a sense of accomplishment.

To address mental clutter, it's essential to develop practices that promote mindfulness, organization, and emotional resilience.

How These Types of Clutter Intersect?

While physical, digital, and mental clutter may seem distinct, they often interact and amplify each other. For instance:

- A cluttered home can lead to feelings of mental overwhelm, making it harder to focus or relax.
- Excessive digital notifications can contribute to mental stress and leave you feeling perpetually distracted.
- Mental clutter, such as procrastination or decision fatigue, can make it difficult to manage physical or digital spaces effectively.

Recognizing how these types of clutter are interconnected is key to addressing them holistically. By taking steps to reduce physical clutter, for example, you may find it easier to focus on digital organization or cultivate a calmer mindset.

The Hidden Costs of Clutter: How It Drains Time, Energy, and Mental Clarity

Clutter often appears innocuous—a messy desk, a crowded inbox, or a mental to-do list that's constantly growing. At first glance, it may seem like something that can be tolerated or ignored. However, clutter is not merely an inconvenience; it comes with significant hidden costs that affect nearly every aspect of our lives. From wasting time and depleting energy to clouding our mental clarity, clutter is a drain on our resources in ways that are often underestimated or overlooked.

1. Clutter Drains Time

One of the most immediate and tangible costs of clutter is the time it steals from us. Whether it's searching for misplaced items, sifting through an overflowing inbox, or trying to make sense of a chaotic schedule, clutter creates inefficiencies that add up over days, weeks, and months.

Lost Time in Physical Spaces

Imagine starting your day by looking for your car keys, only to realize they're buried under a pile of papers on the kitchen counter. The few minutes spent searching might seem insignificant, but when similar instances occur daily, they quickly snowball into hours of wasted time. In fact, studies have shown that the average person spends over 2.5 days per year searching for misplaced items such as phones, wallets, or documents.

Physical clutter also slows down routine tasks. A disorganized kitchen, for example, can turn meal preparation into a stressful and time-consuming ordeal. Similarly, a cluttered workspace can hinder productivity, as time is wasted looking for essential tools or documents needed to complete tasks.

Digital Clutter and the Time Drain

The digital world is not immune to clutter. Many of us lose hours each week dealing with overflowing email inboxes, disorganized files, or irrelevant notifications. Consider the time spent deleting spam emails, scrolling through an endless list of apps, or hunting for a file named "Document_final_v2_revised." Digital clutter not only consumes time directly but also interrupts focus, making it harder to concentrate on meaningful work.

The Decision-Making Bottleneck

Clutter also complicates decision-making, which inherently takes time. For instance, deciding what to wear from an overstuffed closet or choosing which emails to respond to first can create unnecessary delays. These small but frequent decision-making moments, often referred to as "decision fatigue," can drain time and mental energy, leaving us feeling less productive throughout the day.

2. Clutter Depletes Energy

Clutter doesn't just steal time; it also drains energy, often in subtle and insidious ways. This energy depletion affects both our physical stamina and emotional resilience, leaving us feeling exhausted and overwhelmed.

Physical Energy Drain

Living or working in a cluttered environment requires constant physical effort. You may need to move items around to find what you're looking for, clean around piles of stuff, or carry mental notes of where things are located. This ongoing effort to manage clutter can lead to fatigue, as your body and mind expend energy on tasks that could be avoided altogether in a more organized space.

Clutter also creates inefficiencies that force us to exert more effort than necessary. For example, sorting through a stack of disorganized paperwork to find a single document can feel like running a marathon when you're already tired. These repeated instances of wasted energy take a toll over time.

Emotional and Cognitive Energy Drain

The emotional weight of clutter is another hidden energy cost. Cluttered spaces often create a sense of chaos and disarray, which can trigger feelings of frustration, anxiety, or guilt. These emotions drain emotional energy, leaving you less equipped to handle other challenges in your day-to-day life.

Moreover, clutter demands constant mental engagement. Even when you're not actively dealing with it, it sits in the back of your mind as an unresolved issue. This ongoing cognitive engagement, often referred to as "mental load," can be incredibly taxing, reducing your ability to focus on other tasks or recharge effectively.

3. Clutter Erodes Mental Clarity

Perhaps the most profound hidden cost of clutter is its impact on mental clarity. A cluttered environment creates a cluttered mind, making it difficult to think clearly, prioritize tasks, or make sound decisions.

Visual Overstimulation

Physical clutter bombards your senses with unnecessary stimuli, making it harder for your brain to focus. Imagine trying to work in a room filled with stacks of paper, random objects, and half-finished projects. Your brain must constantly filter out these distractions, which takes mental effort and reduces your capacity for deep focus.

Visual clutter is particularly problematic because it sends a subconscious message that there's still work to be done. This creates a low-level sense of stress and urgency, even when you're trying to relax or concentrate.

The Mental Weight of Unfinished Tasks

Clutter often represents unfinished business—things you need to do, decisions you need to make, or items you need to organize. This sense of incompleteness creates mental clutter, filling your mind with thoughts about what you should be doing instead of allowing you to focus on the present.

For example, a cluttered desk might remind you of the report you haven't written, the bills you haven't paid, or the appointments you haven't scheduled. These mental reminders create a constant background noise that clouds your thinking and increases stress.

Reduced Creativity and Problem-Solving

Clutter can also stifle creativity and problem-solving abilities. A disorganized space makes it harder for your brain to draw connections or think innovatively, as it's preoccupied with managing the chaos around you. On the other hand, a clean and organized environment fosters a sense of calm, which can help your mind wander freely and come up with creative ideas.

The hidden costs of clutter don't exist in isolation—they create a ripple effect that impacts other areas of your life. For example:

- Work Productivity: A cluttered workspace can lead to missed deadlines, lower-quality work, and a diminished sense of accomplishment.
- Relationships: Clutter can cause tension in relationships, especially when shared spaces are involved. Disagreements about cleaning or

organizing can strain partnerships, friendships, or family dynamics.

- Health and Well-Being: Clutter contributes to stress, which can manifest as physical symptoms such as headaches, fatigue, or difficulty sleeping. Over time, chronic stress caused by clutter can even lead to more serious health issues, such as high blood pressure or weakened immunity.

The Hidden Opportunity Cost

Finally, it's important to consider the hidden opportunity cost of clutter. Every moment spent dealing with clutter is a moment that could be spent doing something more meaningful or fulfilling. Whether it's pursuing a passion, spending time with loved ones, or simply enjoying a moment of peace, clutter robs us of opportunities to live a richer, more intentional life.

Why We Accumulate Clutter: Unpacking Emotional Attachments, Habits, and Societal Pressures

Clutter does not simply appear overnight. It accumulates gradually, fed by emotional attachments, ingrained habits, and societal influences. Each item we own often holds a deeper significance than its immediate utility, whether it represents memories, aspirations, or societal expectations. Understanding why we accumulate clutter is an essential step toward managing it effectively.

1. Emotional Attachments: When Objects Become More Than Things

Emotional attachment to objects is one of the most powerful reasons clutter builds up in our lives. We often imbue items with meaning far beyond their practical purpose, tying them to our identities, relationships, and past experiences.

Sentimental Value

Objects that remind us of meaningful moments or loved ones are particularly difficult to part with. A box of old letters, a childhood toy, or a souvenir from a memorable trip may hold deep emotional significance, making it feel like discarding the item equates to discarding the memory itself. This attachment to sentimentality often results in keeping items "just in case" or "because they mean something," even if they no longer serve a practical purpose.

For example, you might hold onto a sweater gifted by a late relative, even if it's never worn, because it represents a connection to them. While this emotional tie is natural, it can lead to a build-up of items that serve more as emotional placeholders than functional belongings.

A Sense of Identity

Certain possessions reinforce how we see ourselves or how we wish to be perceived by others. Books, clothing, or hobby-related gear can symbolize an identity we value or aspire to. Even if we no longer engage with a particular hobby or interest, it can be difficult to let go of the items associated with it because they feel tied to our sense of self.

For instance, someone who once loved painting may hold onto unused art supplies, seeing them as a reminder of their creative side—even if they haven't painted in years. Letting go of such items can feel like letting go of a part of themselves.

Guilt and Obligation

We may also keep items out of a sense of guilt or obligation. Gifts, family heirlooms, or items we've spent money on can carry a weight that makes it hard to part with them. The thought of giving away an expensive but unused appliance or discarding a gift from a friend can feel like a betrayal, even if the item serves no practical purpose.

2. Habits That Foster Clutter

While emotions play a significant role, the habits we develop over time also contribute to the accumulation of clutter. These habits often go unnoticed, but they have a profound impact on the state of our physical, digital, and mental spaces.

Impulse Buying

Modern consumer culture thrives on impulse buying, and the convenience of online shopping has only amplified this habit. Sales, discounts, and advertising tap into our desire for instant gratification, encouraging us to buy items we may not need. The result is a steady influx of possessions that accumulate faster than we can use or organize them.

Impulse buying is often driven by emotions such as boredom, stress, or the need for a quick mood boost. The excitement of a new purchase fades quickly, leaving behind items that add to the clutter without adding value to our lives.

Procrastination and Avoidance

Clutter often builds up because we delay decisions about what to keep, donate, or discard. Procrastination leads to piles of unsorted papers, unopened mail, and untouched belongings. This avoidance can stem from a fear of making the "wrong" decision, uncertainty about an item's future value, or simply feeling overwhelmed by the task at hand.

For example, many people keep items they might "someday" need—a broken appliance, outdated technology, or clothing that no longer fits—because they want to avoid regret or additional effort. Over time, these "maybe" items accumulate into significant clutter.

"Just in Case" Thinking

Another habit that fosters clutter is the belief that something might come in handy someday. This mindset often leads to keeping duplicates, outdated items, or things that no longer serve a clear purpose. While it's reasonable to prepare for future needs, holding onto items "just in case" often creates more clutter than it prevents.

3. Societal Pressures: The Culture of Accumulation

Society plays a major role in shaping our relationship with possessions. From marketing messages to cultural norms, external pressures often encourage us to accumulate more than we truly need.

Consumerism and Materialism

Consumer culture promotes the idea that happiness and success are tied to owning more. Advertisements consistently highlight the latest gadgets, trends, and upgrades, creating a sense of urgency to acquire them. Social media amplifies this pressure by showcasing curated images of luxury lifestyles, leading many to feel that owning certain items is essential for status or self-worth.

This constant push to consume can result in purchasing items we don't truly need or want, simply to keep up with societal expectations. Over time, these purchases contribute to clutter, as the items often fail to deliver the satisfaction we hoped for.

The Fear of Missing Out (FOMO)

The fear of missing out also drives accumulation. Limited-time offers, seasonal sales, and the idea that certain items may no longer be available can compel us to buy things we don't need. This FOMO extends beyond physical possessions to digital subscriptions, memberships, and online courses that we may never use but feel compelled to hold onto.

Cultural and Generational Norms

Cultural and generational attitudes toward possessions also influence clutter. In some cultures, keeping items as a symbol of prosperity or tradition is highly valued, making it difficult to let go of things even when they no longer serve a purpose. Similarly, older generations may hold onto items out of a "waste not, want not" mentality, passing down this tendency to younger family members.

4. Psychological Factors at Play

In addition to emotional, habitual, and societal influences, several psychological factors contribute to the accumulation of clutter.

The Endowment Effect

The endowment effect is a cognitive bias where people assign more value to items they own simply because they own them. This makes it harder to part with possessions, even if they are no longer useful or desirable. For example, someone might struggle to discard an old chair they rarely use because they perceive it as more valuable than it objectively is.

Fear of Regret

The fear of regret is another psychological barrier to decluttering. Many people worry they might need an item in the future or regret getting rid of it, leading them to keep things "just in case." This fear often outweighs the practical reality that most items can be replaced if truly needed.

Decision Fatigue

The sheer volume of decisions required to declutter can also contribute to accumulation. Each item represents a choice—keep, donate, recycle, or discard—and this decision-making process can feel overwhelming. As a result, many people avoid the process altogether, allowing clutter to pile up.

5. Breaking the Cycle of Accumulation

Understanding why we accumulate clutter is the first step toward breaking the cycle. Recognizing the emotional, habitual, and societal forces at play allows us to challenge these influences and make more intentional choices.

To combat emotional attachments, it's helpful to focus on the memories associated with an item rather than the item itself. For instance, taking a photo of a sentimental object before donating it can preserve the memory without keeping the clutter.

Addressing habits requires mindfulness and proactive strategies. Avoiding impulse purchases, setting clear limits on what you bring into your space, and committing to regular decluttering sessions can all help reduce accumulation.

Resisting societal pressures involves redefining success and happiness on your own terms. By prioritizing experiences, relationships, and personal growth over material possessions, you can create a life that is rich in meaning rather than cluttered with things.

Chapter 2: Assessing Your Starting Point

Evaluating Your Spaces: Creating an Inventory of Cluttered Areas

Decluttering starts with awareness. Before you can tackle the clutter in your life, it's essential to assess your surroundings and identify the areas that need the most attention. Evaluating your spaces means taking a step back, examining your home or workplace objectively, and understanding the extent of the clutter you're dealing with. This process sets the stage for a focused, effective decluttering journey. One of the most useful tools for this assessment is creating a detailed inventory of cluttered areas. This chapter will guide you through the process, providing practical steps, insights, and tips to help you gain clarity and take control of your environment.

The Importance of Evaluating Your Spaces

It's easy to underestimate how much clutter has accumulated over time. Our eyes often adjust to disorganization, and we might not even notice the extent of the mess until it feels overwhelming. Evaluating your spaces serves several purposes:

- Awareness: You'll gain a clear understanding of where clutter exists and how it impacts your daily life.
- Prioritization: Once you've identified cluttered areas, you can decide where to start based on urgency and impact.
- Focus: Instead of randomly tidying up, you'll have a structured plan for tackling clutter in specific zones.
- Motivation: A comprehensive inventory allows you to track your progress and celebrate small victories as you declutter.

Step 1: Start with a Visual Walkthrough

The first step in evaluating your spaces is to conduct a visual walkthrough of your home or workspace. Grab a notebook or use your phone to jot down notes as you move from room to room. Take your time and observe each area with fresh eyes.

- Look for hotspots: Identify areas that are visibly cluttered, such as piles of papers, overflowing shelves, or drawers that won't close.
- Notice hidden clutter: Don't forget spaces that might be out of sight, like closets, cabinets, under beds, or garage corners.
- Take photos: Sometimes, a photo can reveal details you might overlook during your walkthrough. Compare these images later to track your progress.

Step 2: Categorize Your Spaces

To make your inventory manageable, divide your spaces into categories. This method prevents you from feeling overwhelmed and helps you organize your thoughts. Here are common categories to consider:

Living Spaces:

- Living room, family room, or den.
- Bookshelves, coffee tables, and entertainment centers.
- Décor items and miscellaneous objects.

Kitchen and Dining Areas:

- Countertops, cabinets, and pantry shelves.
- Junk drawers and rarely used gadgets.
- Expired food items or mismatched containers.

Bedrooms:

- Closets, dresser drawers, and bedside tables.
- Laundry piles or seasonal clothing storage.
- Under-the-bed storage.

Bathrooms:

- Cabinets, medicine cabinets, and vanity surfaces.
- Expired toiletries, cosmetics, and cleaning supplies.
- Unused towels or accessories.

Workspaces:

- Desks, file cabinets, and office supplies.
- Digital clutter: computers, tablets, and phones.
- Stacks of paperwork or magazines.

Storage Areas:

- Garages, attics, basements, and sheds.
- Holiday decorations, tools, and sports equipment.

- Forgotten boxes or items saved "just in case."

Miscellaneous Spaces:

- Hallways, entryways, and staircases.
- Car interiors, purses, and backpacks.
- Hobby or craft areas.

Step 3: Identify Pain Points

Once you've categorized your spaces, it's time to dig deeper and identify the areas that cause the most stress or inefficiency. These are your pain points—spaces that frustrate you daily, make it hard to find what you need, or create visual chaos.

Ask yourself questions:

- Which areas do I avoid because they feel overwhelming?
- Where do I waste the most time searching for things?
- Which spaces make me feel stressed or disorganized?
- Look for patterns: Are there specific types of clutter (e.g., clothes, papers, or toys) that appear

in multiple areas? Recognizing these patterns can help you address root causes.

Step 4: Create a Clutter Inventory

Now that you've identified your spaces and pain points, it's time to create a detailed inventory. This inventory serves as a roadmap for your decluttering journey and helps you measure progress over time.

- Use a simple system: Create a list, table, or spreadsheet to document each area. Include columns for:
- Location: The room or space (e.g., bedroom, kitchen).
- Description of Clutter: Specific items or issues (e.g., overflowing closet, unfiled paperwork).
- Priority Level: High, medium, or low based on impact and urgency.
- Action Needed: What needs to happen (e.g., sort, donate, discard).
- Notes: Additional observations or ideas.
- Be specific: Instead of writing "closet," specify "closet – old clothes and shoes." Breaking areas into smaller tasks makes them less intimidating.

Step 5: Use a Clutter Awareness Journal

A clutter awareness journal is a powerful tool for understanding your habits and behaviors around clutter. Use this journal to track your interactions with cluttered spaces over a week or two.

- Record your observations: Write down when and where clutter creates stress, frustration, or inconvenience.
- Reflect on habits: Are there certain times of day or activities that contribute to clutter (e.g., dumping mail on the counter after work)?
- Identify emotional triggers: Note if emotions like guilt, attachment, or indecision play a role in holding onto items.

Step 6: Prioritize Your Spaces

Once your inventory and journal are complete, you'll have a comprehensive overview of your clutter. Use this information to prioritize the spaces you'll tackle first.

- Start with high-impact areas: Focus on spaces that affect your daily life the most, such as the kitchen or bedroom.

- Choose quick wins: Select smaller tasks that can be completed quickly to build momentum and confidence.
- Save sentimental items for later: These can be emotionally challenging, so it's best to address them once you've built your decluttering muscles.

Tips for Staying Motivated

- Set a realistic schedule: Allocate specific times for evaluating and organizing your spaces.
- Celebrate progress: Reward yourself for completing each area, no matter how small.
- Stay patient: Decluttering is a process, not a one-time event. Take it one step at a time.

Identifying Pain Points: Pinpointing Spaces That Cause the Most Stress or Inefficiency

Every space in our home or workplace has a purpose, but when clutter and disorganization creep in, those spaces can become sources of stress and inefficiency. Identifying pain points is a crucial step in understanding where clutter is disrupting your life the most. These are the areas that frustrate you, waste your time, or create unnecessary obstacles in your daily routine. By pinpointing these problem areas, you can prioritize them and develop targeted strategies to transform them into functional, stress-free spaces.

This chapter focuses on recognizing pain points, understanding why they exist, and addressing the emotional and practical challenges they present. Through self-reflection and observation, you can reclaim control over these areas and create a more harmonious environment.

What Are Pain Points?

Pain points are the spaces or systems in your home or workplace that feel overwhelming, inefficient, or stressful. These are the areas where clutter piles up, items get lost, or tasks become unnecessarily complicated. Pain points can vary greatly from person to person, depending on lifestyle, habits, and priorities.

For example:

- A chaotic entryway might make mornings stressful because you can't find your keys or bag.
- An overcrowded closet could waste time every day as you struggle to pick an outfit.

- A cluttered kitchen might make cooking meals feel like a chore rather than an enjoyable activity.

By identifying these pain points, you can prioritize your efforts and focus on solutions that will have the biggest impact on your daily life.

Step 1: Observe Your Daily Routine

The first step in identifying pain points is to pay attention to how you interact with your spaces throughout the day. Take note of the moments when you feel stressed, frustrated, or inefficient.

- Morning Rush: Does your morning routine feel chaotic because you're searching for things like clothes, shoes, or breakfast items?
- Work Tasks: Are you constantly distracted by clutter on your desk, or do you spend time hunting for supplies or documents?
- Evening Wind-Down: Does clutter in the living room or bedroom prevent you from relaxing and unwinding?
- Family Dynamics: Are there spaces where toys, laundry, or other items pile up, causing friction among family members?

Document these moments in a notebook or journal. The goal is to create a map of when and where stress or inefficiency arises in your daily life.

Step 2: Ask the Right Questions

Once you've observed your routine, dive deeper by asking specific questions about your spaces. These questions will help you uncover the root causes of your pain points.

What items do I lose or misplace most often?

- Keys, phones, wallets, or paperwork are common culprits.

What tasks take longer than they should?

- Cooking, cleaning, or getting ready for work might feel unnecessarily time-consuming.

Which spaces do I avoid?

- Areas like closets, garages, or storage rooms might feel too overwhelming to tackle.

What triggers feelings of frustration or stress?

- Think about moments when clutter interferes with your ability to focus or relax.

Step 3: Recognize Common Pain Points

While everyone's pain points are unique, there are some spaces that commonly cause stress and inefficiency. Reviewing these areas might help you identify overlooked problems in your own environment.

Entryways:

- Shoes, bags, and coats piling up by the door.
- No designated spot for keys, mail, or umbrellas.

Closets:

- Clothes you never wear taking up space.
- Difficulty finding items due to overcrowding or poor organization.

Kitchens:

- Countertops cluttered with appliances, utensils, or paperwork.
- Drawers filled with mismatched containers or rarely used gadgets.

Workspaces:

- Desks covered in papers, cables, or random items.

- Poor digital organization (e.g., cluttered email inbox or desktop).

Bathrooms:

- Cabinets overflowing with expired products or unused toiletries.
- Lack of storage for towels, cleaning supplies, or personal care items.

Garages or Storage Areas:

- Tools, decorations, or sports equipment in disarray.
- Boxes of items saved "just in case" but rarely accessed.

Step 4: Analyze Emotional Attachments

Clutter is often tied to emotions, and identifying pain points means acknowledging how these feelings might contribute to the problem.

- Sentimental Items: Do you hold onto things because they remind you of a person, place, or time in your life?

- Guilt: Do you feel bad about discarding items you spent money on, even if they no longer serve a purpose?
- Overwhelm: Does the sheer volume of clutter make it hard to know where to begin?

Understanding these emotional triggers can help you approach decluttering with compassion and clarity.

Step 5: Assess the Impact on Your Life

Once you've identified pain points, evaluate how they affect your overall well-being. Some spaces might be inconvenient but manageable, while others might significantly impact your mental health, productivity, or relationships.

- Time Wasted: How much time do you spend searching for lost items or reorganizing cluttered spaces?
- Stress Levels: Do certain areas make you feel anxious, overwhelmed, or frustrated?
- Lost Opportunities: Does clutter prevent you from fully using your space, such as hosting guests or pursuing hobbies?

Prioritize the spaces that have the most significant impact on your daily life and overall happiness.

Step 6: Create a Plan of Action

Once you've pinpointed your pain points, it's time to develop a plan for addressing them. Start with one area at a time, focusing on spaces that will have the greatest positive impact.

- Break It Down: Divide large areas into smaller, manageable tasks. For example, tackle one kitchen drawer or closet shelf at a time.
- Set Goals: Define what success looks like for each space. Do you want to create more storage, improve accessibility, or simply make it visually pleasing?
- Declutter Strategically: Use the "keep, donate, discard" method to sort through items and reduce clutter.

Step 7: Prevent Future Pain Points

Decluttering is only the first step. To maintain a stress-free environment, implement systems that prevent clutter from building up again.

- Designate Homes for Items: Make sure every item has a specific place where it belongs.
- Adopt Daily Habits: Spend a few minutes each day tidying up high-traffic areas.
- Limit New Clutter: Be mindful of what you bring into your space, and regularly assess whether items are still serving you.

Clutter Awareness Journal: Tracking Patterns and Habits That Contribute to Clutter

Clutter is rarely an accident. More often than not, it results from unconscious habits, unexamined patterns, and a lack of awareness about how we interact with our spaces. To address clutter effectively, it's essential to understand its root causes, which go beyond simply acquiring too many things. By keeping a clutter awareness journal, you can identify the habits and behaviours contributing to disorganization, track patterns over time, and take meaningful steps toward creating a clutter-free environment.

A clutter awareness journal is not just a notebook for jotting down observations; it's a powerful tool for self-reflection and change. It helps you explore your relationship with your belongings, identify triggers that lead to clutter, and uncover emotional or psychological barriers to maintaining a tidy space.

Why Keep a Clutter Awareness Journal?

A clutter awareness journal provides insight into the "why" behind your clutter. While decluttering often focuses on the physical act of removing items, understanding the underlying patterns is key to preventing clutter from returning.

Here are some reasons why a clutter awareness journal is invaluable:

- Spotting Patterns: You might notice recurring clutter hotspots or habits, such as always leaving mail on the kitchen counter or neglecting to put shoes away.
- Identifying Triggers: Emotional or situational triggers, such as stress, boredom, or impulse shopping, can contribute to clutter.
- Promoting Mindfulness: Writing about your interactions with your space makes you more conscious of your behaviours and choices.

- Setting Goals: By documenting your observations, you can create realistic and specific goals to tackle clutter over time.

How to Set Up Your Clutter Awareness Journal

Your clutter awareness journal doesn't need to be fancy—it can be a simple notebook, a digital document, or even a dedicated section in a planner. What matters is consistency and intentionality in using it.

Choose Your Format:

- Physical Journal: A notebook allows for freeform writing and doodling.
- Digital Option: Apps like Notion, Evernote, or a simple Word document can be used for more structured tracking.
- Hybrid Approach: Use both a physical and digital format if it suits your style.

Decide on Categories:

- Common categories to track include specific rooms (kitchen, bedroom, office), recurring clutter types (clothes, papers, toys), and habits (shopping, tidying routines).

- Leave space for emotional insights, such as how the clutter makes you feel and what thoughts arise when you confront it.

Create Prompts:

Use prompts to guide your entries, such as:

- "What clutter did I notice today, and where was it located?"
- "What habits led to this clutter? (e.g., not putting things back after use)"
- "How did the clutter make me feel, and how did it impact my day?"
- "What steps can I take to address or prevent this clutter?"

Set a Schedule:

- Aim to write in your journal daily or at least a few times a week. Regular entries will help you identify patterns more effectively.

What to Track in Your Clutter Awareness Journal?

To gain meaningful insights, focus on tracking both the physical and emotional aspects of clutter. Here are some key areas to document:

1. Clutter Hotspots

- Identify areas in your home or workplace that accumulate clutter most frequently.
- Examples: the dining table, the nightstand, or the garage.

2. Daily Habits

- Note specific behaviours that lead to clutter, such as leaving dishes in the sink or tossing clothes on a chair.
- Example entry: "Left groceries on the counter for hours instead of putting them away right away."

3. Triggers

- Document events, emotions, or situations that lead to clutter accumulation.
- Example entry: "Felt stressed after work, so I dumped my bag and coat on the couch instead of hanging them up."

4. Impact of Clutter

- Reflect on how the clutter affects your mood, productivity, or relationships.

- Example entry: "Seeing my messy desk made me feel overwhelmed and unmotivated to start working."

5. Progress and Wins

- Celebrate small victories, such as clearing a countertop or organizing a drawer.
- Example entry: "Organized my closet today and donated 10 items I no longer wear. Felt lighter afterward!"

Uncovering Patterns and Habits

After a few weeks of journaling, review your entries to identify patterns and habits. Here are some common themes you might uncover:

Recurring Clutter Zones:

- Certain areas, like entryways or kitchen counters, tend to attract clutter repeatedly.
- Solution: Create dedicated storage solutions for these zones, such as hooks for keys or bins for mail.

Procrastination:

- You may notice a habit of delaying small tasks, such as folding laundry or putting away groceries.
- Solution: Adopt the "one-minute rule" for tasks that take less than a minute to complete.

Impulse Purchases:

- Shopping without a plan may lead to unnecessary items that pile up at home.
- Solution: Implement a 24-hour rule before buying non-essential items.

Emotional Triggers:

- Stress, boredom, or sadness might lead to behaviours like leaving items out or acquiring more things.
- Solution: Develop healthier coping mechanisms, such as journaling, exercising, or meditating.

Using Your Journal to Create Change

Once you've identified patterns and habits, use your clutter awareness journal as a roadmap for creating positive change.

1. Set Specific Goals

- Based on your observations, set targeted goals for addressing clutter.
- Example: "By the end of the month, I will clear and organize the dining table and establish a system for incoming mail."

2. Experiment with Solutions

- Test different strategies to see what works best for you.
- Example: "This week, I'll set a timer for 10 minutes every evening to tidy up the living room."

3. Reflect on Progress

- Regularly review your journal to track improvements and identify new challenges.
- Example: "Clearing my desk every evening has helped me start each workday feeling more focused."

4. Stay Accountable

- Share your goals with a friend, family member, or accountability partner.

The Emotional Benefits of Clutter Awareness

Journaling about clutter isn't just about physical organization—it's also a way to process the emotional and mental impact of your environment. By confronting the feelings associated with clutter, you can:

- Reduce Stress: Writing about clutter-related frustrations can help you release pent-up emotions.
- Gain Clarity: Reflecting on your habits can provide a sense of control and direction.
- Boost Confidence: Celebrating small wins boosts your motivation and self-esteem.

Long-Term Benefits of a Clutter Awareness Journal

Over time, your clutter awareness journal will become a valuable resource for maintaining a clutter-free lifestyle. It can:

- Prevent Relapses: By recognizing the habits that lead to clutter, you can take proactive steps to avoid falling back into old patterns.
- Promote Mindfulness: Journaling helps you stay conscious of your relationship with your possessions and environment.

- Foster Growth: Tracking your progress reinforces the positive changes you've made and inspires continued improvement.

Chapter 3: Shifting Your Mindset

Letting Go of Perfectionism: Embracing Progress Over Perfection

Perfectionism often masquerades as a virtue. It whispers promises of excellence and high achievement, but in reality, it can trap us in a cycle of self-doubt, procrastination, and paralyzing fear of failure. While striving for excellence is commendable, perfectionism takes this to an unhealthy extreme, where even the smallest flaws feel unacceptable and every endeavor becomes a test of one's worth. Letting go of perfectionism and embracing progress over perfection is not only liberating but also essential for personal growth, mental well-being, and productivity.

The Illusion of Perfection

At its core, perfectionism is rooted in the illusion that flawlessness is achievable. This belief often stems from societal pressures, cultural norms, and personal insecurities. Social media exacerbates this by presenting curated images of ideal lives, flawless workspaces, and unattainable standards. As a result, many feel compelled to live up to these unrealistic expectations, even if it means sacrificing their mental health.

What perfectionists often fail to recognize is that perfection is subjective. What seems perfect to one person may fall short to another. Additionally, striving for perfection in every area of life is neither sustainable nor realistic. This pursuit can lead to burnout, dissatisfaction, and a sense of failure when the unattainable remains out of reach.

How Perfectionism Holds Us Back

- Procrastination and Fear of Failure: Perfectionists often delay starting tasks out of fear that they won't meet their high standards. This leads to procrastination, which further increases anxiety and stress. The fear of failure becomes so overwhelming that taking any action feels impossible.
- Reduced Productivity: The obsession with every detail being flawless can lead to overthinking and wasted time. Instead of completing a task efficiently, perfectionists may spend hours tweaking minor details, which can stall progress and reduce overall productivity.

- Damaged Self-Esteem: Perfectionism often involves setting impossible standards for oneself. When these standards aren't met, feelings of inadequacy, guilt, and shame take over. This creates a cycle of self-criticism that erodes self-esteem over time.

- Strained Relationships: The perfectionist mindset doesn't just affect individuals—it spills over into relationships. Perfectionists may project their unrealistic standards onto others, causing frustration and tension. They may also struggle to delegate tasks, fearing that others won't meet their exacting standards.

Shifting the Mindset: Embracing Progress Over Perfection

Letting go of perfectionism requires a mindset shift: from seeing mistakes as failures to viewing them as opportunities for growth, and from fixating on the end result to appreciating the journey. Embracing progress over perfection can help individuals achieve more, feel more fulfilled, and experience a greater sense of freedom in life.

1. Redefine Success

Start by challenging the idea that success equals flawlessness. Instead, define success as consistent improvement, effort, and growth. Celebrate small victories, acknowledge the progress you've made, and recognize that perfection is not a requirement for success.

Example: Instead of saying, "I need to create the perfect presentation," aim for, "I want to create a presentation that effectively communicates my ideas." This shift allows you to focus on the purpose of the task rather than its perceived perfection.

2. Practice Self-Compassion

Perfectionists are often their harshest critics. Practicing self-compassion involves treating yourself with the same kindness and understanding you would offer a friend. When you make a mistake, instead of berating yourself, acknowledge that errors are a natural part of learning and growing.

Mantra: "I am doing my best, and that is enough."

3. Focus on the Process

Progress is about taking small, consistent steps toward your goals. Shift your focus from the end result to the process itself. By concentrating on the effort you put in, you'll find joy in the journey rather than stressing over the outcome.

Practical Tip: Set process-based goals, such as "I will write for 30 minutes every day," rather than outcome-based goals like "I will finish the perfect chapter by Friday."

4. Embrace Imperfection as Growth

Mistakes and imperfections are not failures; they're valuable lessons. Each misstep offers an opportunity to learn, adapt, and improve. The most successful individuals often credit their failures as pivotal moments that led to growth and innovation.

Mindset Shift: Replace "What if I fail?" with "What can I learn from this?"

5. Set Realistic Standards

Perfectionists often set impossibly high standards for themselves and others. Learn to differentiate between high-quality work and perfection. Aim for excellence where it matters and give yourself permission to be "good enough" in areas where perfection is unnecessary.

Example: For a work project, identify key areas that require attention to detail and let go of less critical elements.

Practical Strategies for Letting Go of Perfectionism

- Start Before You're Ready: Waiting for the perfect moment or conditions often leads to inaction. Instead, take imperfect action. Starting is more important than waiting to feel fully prepared. Mantra: "Done is better than perfect."

- Set Time Limits: Give yourself a set amount of time to complete a task. This prevents overthinking and helps you prioritize efficiency over perfection. Example: "I'll spend 90 minutes on this report and then move on, even if it's not perfect."

- Prioritize What Matters: Not everything requires the same level of effort or attention. Identify what tasks truly require high standards and which ones can be approached with a "good enough" mindset.

Tool: Use the Eisenhower Matrix to categorize tasks by urgency and importance.

- Seek Feedback: Instead of aiming for perfection in isolation, seek feedback from trusted individuals. They can offer fresh perspectives and help you identify areas for improvement without the pressure of perfectionism.

- Celebrate Progress: Keep a journal of your achievements, no matter how small. Reflecting on progress over time can help you appreciate how far you've come and reduce the fixation on perfection.

The Benefits of Embracing Progress Over Perfection

- Increased Productivity: By focusing on progress, you can complete tasks more efficiently without being bogged down by unnecessary details.

- Enhanced Creativity: Letting go of the need for perfection frees you to take risks and experiment. This fosters creativity and innovation, as you're no longer afraid to fail.

- Improved Mental Health: Releasing the pressure to be perfect reduces stress, anxiety, and self-criticism, leading to greater emotional well-being.

- Greater Fulfilment: Focusing on progress allows you to enjoy the journey, celebrate small wins, and feel a sense of accomplishment along the way.
- Stronger Relationships: By letting go of unrealistic expectations, you can cultivate more authentic and supportive connections with others.

Adopting a Minimalist Mindset: Understanding Its Benefits and Practical Application

Consumer-driven world, the pursuit of more often leads to stress, distraction, and a cluttered life. Minimalism offers an antidote to this chaos, advocating for a mindset that focuses on living with intention and simplicity. While often associated with decluttering physical possessions, minimalism extends far beyond the material. It's about shifting priorities, valuing quality over quantity, and creating space for what truly matters. Adopting a minimalist mindset can bring profound benefits to mental health, relationships, productivity, and overall well-being.

What Is a Minimalist Mindset?

At its core, a minimalist mindset is about intentionally focusing on what adds value to your life while letting go of the excess. It's not about deprivation or living with the bare minimum—it's about clarity and purpose. Minimalism encourages you to strip away the unnecessary, whether it's physical clutter, toxic relationships, or mental distractions, to make room for what truly aligns with your goals and values.

Minimalism is not one-size-fits-all. For some, it might mean owning fewer belongings, while for others, it might involve simplifying schedules, commitments, or even digital consumption. The beauty of minimalism is that it's highly personal and adaptable to individual needs.

Benefits of Adopting a Minimalist Mindset

1. Mental Clarity and Reduced Stress

Clutter, whether physical or mental, can overwhelm the senses and increase stress. A minimalist mindset helps reduce this noise by eliminating unnecessary distractions. With fewer things demanding your attention, you can focus on what truly matters, leading to greater mental clarity and peace of mind.

2. Increased Productivity

Minimalism encourages you to prioritize your time and energy on tasks that align with your goals. By saying "no" to distractions and nonessential commitments, you free up mental and emotional bandwidth to excel in areas that matter most.

3. Financial Freedom

A minimalist lifestyle often involves rethinking spending habits and resisting the urge to accumulate material possessions. This shift can lead to significant financial savings, reduced debt, and greater freedom to invest in experiences or long-term goals.

4. Stronger Relationships

Minimalism can extend to relationships by encouraging intentional connections. By letting go of toxic or superficial relationships, you can focus on nurturing meaningful bonds with the people who truly matter.

5. Environmental Impact

Minimalism often promotes sustainable living by reducing waste and unnecessary consumption.

6. Deeper Fulfilment

Minimalism shifts the focus from external validation to internal contentment. By prioritizing experiences, personal growth, and connections over material goods, you can find deeper satisfaction and a greater sense of purpose.

Practical Applications of a Minimalist Mindset

Embracing minimalism doesn't require a complete overhaul of your life overnight. Small, intentional steps can help you transition into a minimalist mindset while making meaningful changes.

1. Declutter Your Physical Space

Physical clutter often reflects mental clutter. Start by decluttering your home, workspace, or any area that feels overwhelming.

- The KonMari Method: Ask yourself if each item brings you joy or serves a purpose. If not, let it go.
- One-In-One-Out Rule: For every new item you bring into your home, let go of an old one to maintain balance.

- Room-by-Room Approach: Tackle one room or area at a time to avoid feeling overwhelmed.

Decluttering doesn't mean owning nothing—it means owning only what adds value to your life.

2. Simplify Your Schedule

Overcommitting to tasks, events, and obligations can lead to burnout. Adopt a minimalist approach to your time by learning to prioritize and say no.

- Time Blocking: Allocate specific blocks of time for essential tasks and rest.
- The 80/20 Rule: Focus on the 20% of activities that yield 80% of your results.
- Cutting Nonessentials: Review your commitments and eliminate activities that don't align with your priorities.

3. Revaluate Spending Habits

Minimalism often involves being intentional with finances. Ask yourself whether each purchase aligns with your values and long-term goals.

- Quality Over Quantity: Invest in durable, high-quality items that last, rather than cheap, disposable products.
- Mindful Consumption: Delay purchases by 24–48 hours to determine whether they're truly necessary.
- Budgeting for Priorities: Allocate more of your income to experiences, savings, or personal growth instead of material goods.

4. Practice Digital Minimalism

The digital age has brought unprecedented access to information but also constant distraction. Apply a minimalist mindset to your digital life.

- Declutter Devices: Organize files, delete unused apps, and unsubscribe from unnecessary emails or notifications.
- Limit Screen Time: Set boundaries for social media and digital consumption to reclaim time for meaningful activities.

- Focus on Intentional Use: Use technology as a tool to support your goals rather than a source of mindless distraction.

5. Cultivate a Mindful Mindset

Minimalism and mindfulness often go hand in hand. Mindfulness involves being present and intentional in your actions, which aligns seamlessly with a minimalist lifestyle.

- Daily Reflection: Spend a few minutes each day reflecting on what's truly important.
- Gratitude Practice: Shift your focus from what you lack to appreciating what you have.
- Mindful Decision-Making: Pause before making decisions to consider whether they align with your values.

6. Simplify Relationships

Focus on quality over quantity in your relationships. Surround yourself with people who uplift and inspire you, and let go of relationships that drain your energy or no longer serve you.

- Prioritize Connection: Spend more time with loved ones and engage in meaningful conversations.
- Set Boundaries: Protect your time and energy by saying no to toxic or draining interactions.

Challenges of Adopting a Minimalist Mindset

While the benefits of minimalism are significant, the journey isn't always easy. Letting go of material possessions or habits that no longer serve you can be emotionally challenging. Fear of missing out (FOMO), societal pressures, and the initial discomfort of change can create resistance.

However, these challenges can be overcome with patience and a gradual approach. Remind yourself of the long-term benefits, and take small, manageable steps. Minimalism is a journey, not a destination.

Minimalism Is Not About Perfection

It's important to note that minimalism itself doesn't require perfection. The goal is not to live with as little as possible but to live with intention. Some days may feel cluttered, and that's okay. Minimalism is about progress, not strict rules.

It's also deeply personal. What feels minimal for one person may look excessive to another, and that's perfectly fine. Your version of minimalism should reflect your unique values, goals, and lifestyle.

Overcoming Emotional Barriers: Addressing Guilt and Sentimental Attachments

Emotions play a significant role in shaping how we perceive and navigate the world. While positive emotions often serve as motivators, negative ones—such as guilt and sentimental attachments—can sometimes become barriers, holding us back from growth, progress, and fulfillment. Overcoming these emotional barriers requires deep introspection, understanding, and the development of strategies to address the root causes of guilt and sentimental attachment.

Understanding Emotional Barriers

An emotional barrier is a psychological block that prevents someone from taking action, making decisions, or moving forward in life. These barriers are often rooted in unresolved emotions such as guilt, fear, shame, or an excessive attachment to past experiences or people.

What Is Guilt?

Guilt is the feeling of responsibility or remorse for an action (or inaction) that is perceived as wrong. While guilt can be a healthy emotion when it drives accountability and reparative action, it becomes a barrier when it is unresolved or irrational. Excessive guilt can lead to self-blame, low self-esteem, and a tendency to avoid confronting difficult situations.

What Are Sentimental Attachments?

Sentimental attachments involve an emotional bond to people, objects, or memories. While these attachments can bring comfort and nostalgia, they can also become barriers when they prevent us from letting go of things that no longer serve us. For example, holding onto possessions that remind us of the past, even when they create clutter, is a common manifestation of sentimental attachment.

How Guilt and Sentimental Attachments Hold Us Back

1. Guilt Creates Emotional Paralysis

When guilt becomes overwhelming, it often leads to inaction. People may feel stuck in a cycle of self-recrimination, unable to forgive themselves or others. This can manifest as procrastination, avoidance of responsibilities, or an inability to make decisions.

For example, someone who feels guilty about a failed relationship may avoid pursuing new connections for fear of repeating the past. Similarly, guilt about not living up to personal or societal expectations can prevent individuals from embracing opportunities that align with their authentic selves.

2. Sentimental Attachments Prevent Progress

Holding onto sentimental attachments can make it difficult to move forward. Whether it's a box of keepsakes from a former partner, an old career path, or a home filled with objects from the past, these attachments often anchor us in a place of stagnation.

By clinging to the past, we may inadvertently block the possibility of new experiences, relationships, and personal growth. The emotional weight of these attachments can also lead to feelings of overwhelm and stress, especially when they become a source of clutter or disorganization.

3. Both Can Impact Mental Health

Unchecked guilt and sentimental attachments can take a toll on mental health. Guilt can lead to chronic stress, anxiety, and depression, while sentimental attachments can evoke feelings of loss, sadness, or frustration when letting go feels impossible. Together, they can create a cycle of emotional exhaustion that affects overall well-being.

Steps to Overcome Guilt

1. Acknowledge and Understand the Source of Guilt

The first step to overcoming guilt is acknowledging its presence and identifying its root cause. Ask yourself:

- What am I feeling guilty about?
- Is my guilt rational or irrational?
- Did I intentionally cause harm, or am I holding myself to an unrealistic standard?

Sometimes, guilt arises from internalized societal or cultural expectations rather than genuine wrongdoing.

Distinguishing between productive and unproductive guilt can help you address it more effectively.

2. Practice Self-Forgiveness

Self-forgiveness is a crucial step in overcoming guilt. Recognize that you are human and capable of making mistakes. Holding onto guilt indefinitely doesn't serve you or others.

- Acknowledge Your Imperfections: Embrace the fact that mistakes are part of growth.
- Make Amends: If your guilt stems from harm caused to someone else, take steps to apologize and repair the situation if possible.
- Reframe the Narrative: Focus on what you've learned from the experience rather than dwelling on regret.

3. Challenge Negative Self-Talk

Guilt often fuels a cycle of negative self-talk, where you constantly criticize yourself. Challenge these thoughts by reframing them into more compassionate and constructive statements.

- Instead of saying, "I'm a terrible person for making this mistake," try, "I made a mistake, but I'm taking steps to make things right."

4. Focus on the Present

Guilt often ties us to the past, but focusing on the present can help break free from its grip. Practice mindfulness techniques, such as meditation or deep breathing, to ground yourself in the here and now.

5. Seek Support

If guilt feels overwhelming, seek support from a trusted friend, family member, or therapist. Talking about your feelings can provide clarity and help you process them more effectively.

Steps to Overcome Sentimental Attachments

1. Assess the Value of What You're Holding Onto

When dealing with sentimental attachments, ask yourself whether the object, memory, or relationship still adds value to your life.

- Does it Bring Joy? If an item or memory brings genuine happiness or comfort, it may be worth keeping.
- Does it Serve a Purpose? If it no longer serves a practical or emotional purpose, consider letting it go.

2. Start Small

Letting go of sentimental attachments can feel daunting, so start small. Begin with one drawer, box, or area of your life and gradually work your way through.

3. Preserve Memories in Nonphysical Ways

You don't have to hold onto physical objects to preserve memories. Consider taking photos, creating a digital scrapbook, or writing about the memory in a journal. This allows you to honor the past without being weighed down by material possessions.

4. Embrace the Idea of Impermanence

Recognize that life is constantly changing and that holding onto the past can hinder your ability to embrace the present and future.

- Reflect on the impermanence of all things and remind yourself that letting go doesn't mean forgetting—it means making room for new opportunities.

5. Seek Professional Help if Needed

If sentimental attachments are deeply rooted in unresolved trauma or loss, consider working with a therapist to address the underlying emotions.

Strategies for Both Guilt and Sentimental Attachments

1. Practice Gratitude

Gratitude can help shift your focus from what you've lost to what you have. Regularly reflect on the people, experiences, and opportunities that bring you joy and fulfillment.

2. Set Boundaries

Whether it's with yourself or others, setting boundaries can help you manage guilt and sentimental attachments. For example, decide how much time or energy you're willing to invest in revisiting the past and stick to those limits.

3. Embrace Minimalism

Minimalism isn't just about decluttering possessions— it's a mindset that encourages letting go of what no longer serves you. By embracing minimalism, you can free yourself from the emotional weight of guilt and sentimental attachments.

4. Celebrate Progress

Overcoming emotional barriers is a journey, not a destination. Celebrate small victories along the way, whether it's forgiving yourself for a mistake or letting go of a sentimental item.

Chapter 4: Setting Clear Goals and Priorities

Defining Your Vision: Imagining and Articulating Your Ideal Clutter-Free Life

The process of decluttering starts long before you pick up a box or sort through your closet. It begins with a vision—a clear, compelling picture of what your ideal clutter-free life looks like. This vision serves as your guiding light, keeping you motivated and on track as you navigate the sometimes challenging process of letting go. Without a vision, decluttering can feel like an endless chore; with one, it transforms into an intentional journey toward a more fulfilling, peaceful life.

Why Define Your Vision?

Decluttering isn't just about removing physical items from your space—it's about creating an environment that aligns with your values, goals, and the way you want to live. A well-defined vision helps you:

- Stay Focused: When you know what you're working toward, it's easier to make decisions about what to keep and what to let go of.

- Overcome Challenges: Letting go of certain items can be emotionally difficult. A clear vision reminds you why the effort is worthwhile.
- Create Lasting Change: Without a vision, decluttering may only address surface-level issues. A strong sense of purpose ensures that your efforts lead to sustainable habits.

Envisioning Your Clutter-Free Life

Imagining your ideal life without clutter requires self-reflection and creativity. Here's how to start:

1. Picture Your Perfect Space

Close your eyes and imagine walking into your home. What does it look like? Is it open and airy, with clean surfaces and carefully chosen décor? Are your closets and drawers organized, making it easy to find what you need? Picture every detail: the colors, the layout, and even how the space makes you feel.

Think about specific rooms:

- In the living room, perhaps there's no pile of magazines or tangled cords—just a comfortable space for relaxation or connection with loved ones.

- In the kitchen, imagine counters free of clutter, with only the essentials neatly stored away.
- In the bedroom, see a calm, serene sanctuary that promotes rest and rejuvenation.

The goal is to create a mental image of a home that supports your lifestyle and brings you joy.

2. Identify How You Want to Feel

Clutter-free living isn't just about aesthetics; it's about how your environment influences your emotional and mental well-being. Ask yourself:

- Do I want to feel more peaceful and less overwhelmed?
- Do I want my space to inspire creativity and productivity?
- Do I want to feel proud to invite guests into my home?

Write down the feelings you want to cultivate. For example:

- "I want to feel calm when I walk through my front door."
- "I want to wake up in a bedroom that feels serene and restful."
- "I want to feel productive and focused in my home office."

These emotions will help guide your decisions as you declutter.

3. Consider Your Values and Priorities

Your ideal clutter-free life should reflect your unique values and priorities. Take some time to think about what matters most to you. For instance:

- If family is a top priority, you might envision a home with open spaces for gathering and playing together.
- If you value creativity, you might picture a studio or workspace free of distractions, where you can focus on your projects.
- If you cherish simplicity, you might imagine a minimalist aesthetic with fewer belongings and more space to breathe.

Aligning your vision with your values ensures that your decluttered life feels authentic and fulfilling.

Articulating Your Vision

Once you've imagined your ideal clutter-free life, the next step is to articulate it clearly. Writing it down makes your vision tangible and actionable. Follow these steps to craft a clear statement:

1. Write a Vision Statement

Create a short, powerful description of your ideal life. Use positive, present-tense language to make it feel real and achievable. For example:

- "I live in a home that feels light, peaceful, and welcoming. Everything I own has a purpose or brings me joy, and my spaces are organized to support my daily routines."

Keep your statement concise and inspiring. It should motivate you whenever you read it.

2. Set Specific Goals

Break your vision into smaller, actionable goals. For example:

- "Create a clutter-free kitchen where I can cook without distractions."
- "Transform my bedroom into a restful space with only the essentials."
- "Organize my home office to boost productivity and creativity."

These goals give you a roadmap to follow as you work through each area of your home.

3. Use Visual Tools

If you're a visual learner, consider creating a vision board. Gather images from magazines, Pinterest, or other sources that represent your ideal space. Include words or phrases that capture the feelings and values you want your home to embody. Place your vision board somewhere you'll see it often, like your workspace or refrigerator, to keep you motivated.

Bringing Your Vision to Life

With your vision defined and articulated, it's time to start aligning your environment with your goals. Here are some practical tips to help:

1. Start Small

Begin with a single room, area, or category of items. For example, tackle your kitchen counter or a single drawer before moving on to larger projects. Starting small builds momentum and gives you a sense of accomplishment.

2. Use Your Vision as a Compass

Whenever you're unsure about whether to keep or discard an item, refer back to your vision. Ask yourself:

- Does this item support the life I want to create?
- Does it align with the feelings I want to cultivate in my home?

If the answer is no, it's time to let it go.

3. Celebrate Progress

As you declutter, take time to acknowledge your achievements. Reflect on how your space is beginning to align with your vision. Celebrating progress keeps you motivated and reinforces the benefits of your efforts.

The Impact of a Clear Vision

Defining your vision isn't just a step in the decluttering process—it's a transformative exercise in itself. By imagining and articulating your ideal clutter-free life, you gain clarity about what truly matters to you. This clarity extends beyond your physical environment, influencing your mindset, habits, and priorities in other areas of life.

When you live in alignment with your vision, you'll experience:

- Reduced Stress: A clutter-free environment creates a sense of calm and order.
- Increased Productivity: With fewer distractions, it's easier to focus and get things done.
- Greater Joy: Surrounding yourself with items that bring you happiness enhances your overall quality of life.
- Freedom to Grow: Letting go of unnecessary possessions frees up time, energy, and resources to pursue your passions and goals.

Your vision is the foundation of a clutter-free life. It gives purpose to your actions, helps you overcome obstacles, and keeps you moving forward. As you bring your vision to life, you'll discover that decluttering is about much more than organizing your space—it's about creating a life that reflects your values and allows you to thrive.

So take the time to dream big, reflect deeply, and define a vision that inspires you. Your ideal clutter-free life is within reach, and it all starts with a clear and compelling picture of what you want to achieve.

Creating SMART Goals: Clear and Actionable Steps to Achieve Your Vision

Defining your vision is a powerful first step toward transforming your life, but without a plan of action, even the clearest vision can remain just a dream. That's where SMART goals come in. The SMART framework—Specific, Measurable, Achievable, Relevant, and Time-bound—provides a structured approach to breaking your vision into actionable steps. By creating SMART goals, you can chart a clear path toward success, stay motivated, and measure your progress along the way.

Why SMART Goals Work

SMART goals turn abstract aspirations into tangible actions. They force you to clarify what you want, ensure that your goals are realistic, and provide a clear timeline for completion. This method works because it:

- Promotes Clarity: SMART goals remove ambiguity, making it easier to focus on what truly matters.
- Increases Motivation: Clear, actionable steps help you see progress, keeping you inspired.
- Encourages Accountability: With measurable milestones, it's easier to hold yourself accountable and stay on track.
- Supports Long-Term Success: By breaking big dreams into manageable tasks, SMART goals create sustainable progress.

Breaking Down the SMART Framework

1. Specific: Define Clear, Concrete Goals

A vague goal like "declutter my home" can feel overwhelming because it lacks focus. The first step in the SMART process is to make your goal specific by answering these questions:

- What exactly do I want to achieve?
- Why is this goal important to me?
- Where will I focus my efforts?

For example, instead of saying, "I want to organize my home," a specific goal might be: "I will declutter my kitchen by organizing the pantry, clearing the countertops, and donating unused appliances."

The more detailed your goal, the easier it is to take action.

2. Measurable: Define Success in Quantifiable Terms

How will you know when you've achieved your goal? Adding measurable criteria ensures you can track progress and celebrate milestones.

Ask yourself:

- How much?
- How many?
- How will I know when the goal is accomplished?

Building on the previous example, a measurable goal might be: "I will reduce the number of items in my kitchen pantry by 50% and clear all countertops of unnecessary items."

Tracking your progress keeps you motivated and helps you identify areas where you may need to adjust your efforts.

3. Achievable: Set Realistic, Attainable Goals

While it's important to dream big, your goals should also be realistic. Setting unattainable goals can lead to frustration and burnout.

To ensure your goals are achievable, consider:

- Do I have the resources, time, and skills to accomplish this goal?
- What obstacles might I face, and how can I overcome them?
- Can I break this goal into smaller, more manageable steps?

For instance, if your vision is to declutter your entire home, an achievable starting point might be: "I will declutter one room each week, starting with the kitchen."

This approach ensures steady progress without overwhelming yourself.

4. Relevant: Align Goals with Your Vision and Values

Your goals should reflect what truly matters to you and support your broader vision. Setting goals that align with your priorities ensures you stay motivated and committed.

Ask yourself:

- Does this goal align with my long-term vision?
- Is this goal meaningful and important to me?
- Will achieving this goal bring me closer to the life I want to create?

For example, if your vision is to create a peaceful, organized home, a relevant goal might be: "I will declutter my bedroom to create a calming space for rest and relaxation."

By focusing on goals that resonate with your values, you'll find it easier to stay on track.

5. Time-Bound: Establish a Clear Deadline

A goal without a deadline is just a wish. Adding a time frame creates a sense of urgency and helps you prioritize your efforts.

Consider:

- When do I want to achieve this goal?
- What milestones can I set along the way?
- Is this timeline realistic and manageable?

For example, a time-bound goal might be: "I will declutter my kitchen by the end of the month, focusing on one section each week: the pantry in Week 1, the countertops in Week 2, and the cabinets in Week 3."

Having a deadline ensures you maintain momentum and avoid procrastination.

Creating SMART Goals: A Step-by-Step Guide

Now that we've broken down the SMART framework, let's apply it to your life. Follow these steps to create and implement effective goals:

Step 1: Start with Your Vision

Review your vision for a clutter-free life. What does success look like to you? Use this vision as the foundation for setting your goals.

Step 2: Prioritize Key Areas

Identify the areas of your life or home that need the most attention. For example, you might focus on decluttering your workspace to improve productivity or organizing your living room to create a more welcoming space.

Step 3: Write SMART Goals

Using the SMART criteria, write clear, actionable goals for each priority area. For instance:

- Specific: "I will organize my bedroom closet by sorting clothes into keep, donate, and discard piles."
- Measurable: "I will reduce the number of items in my closet by 40%."
- Achievable: "I will dedicate two hours every Saturday to this task."
- Relevant: "This aligns with my vision of a clutter-free, peaceful bedroom."
- Time-bound: "I will complete this goal within four weeks."

Step 4: Break Goals into Actionable Steps

Divide each goal into smaller tasks. For example, the goal to declutter your closet might include steps like:

- Empty the closet and sort items into categories.
- Try on clothes and assess fit and condition.
- Donate or discard items you no longer need.
- Organize remaining items by type and season.

Breaking goals into steps makes them less intimidating and more manageable.

Step 5: Track Your Progress

Keep a journal, checklist, or digital tracker to monitor your progress. Celebrate small wins along the way, like completing one section of a room or donating a box of items.

Step 6: Adjust as Needed

Life is unpredictable, and your goals may need to evolve. If you encounter obstacles, reassess your plan and adjust your timeline or approach. The key is to stay flexible and persistent.

Examples of SMART Goals for a Clutter-Free Life

Here are a few examples to inspire your own goals:

Goal: "I will create a functional home office by organizing my desk, filing papers, and clearing out unused supplies."

- Timeline: Two weeks.
- Steps: Dedicate 30 minutes each day to sorting and organizing.

Goal: "I will declutter my digital life by organizing my email inbox, deleting old files, and backing up important documents."

- Timeline: One month.
- Steps: Spend 15 minutes each morning tackling one digital category.

Goal: "I will establish a system for maintaining a clutter-free home by implementing daily cleaning habits and monthly donation drives."

- Timeline: Start immediately and review progress in six months.
- Steps: Create a checklist of daily and monthly tasks.

Staying Motivated with SMART Goals

Even with SMART goals, staying motivated can be challenging. Here are some tips to keep your momentum:

- Visualize Success: Regularly revisit your vision to remind yourself why you started.
- Reward Progress: Celebrate milestones with small rewards, like a new organizer or a relaxing evening off.

- Seek Support: Share your goals with friends or family and ask for encouragement or accountability.
- Focus on the Benefits: Reflect on how your life is improving as you declutter and organize.

Identifying Priority Areas: Focusing on High-Impact Areas to Start Your Journey

Embarking on a transformative journey, whether it's decluttering your home, achieving a life goal, or improving your overall well-being, requires knowing where to focus your energy first. Identifying priority areas is crucial because not all tasks or areas have the same level of impact. Focusing on high-priority areas creates momentum, builds confidence, and allows you to see tangible results early in the process. This clarity ensures that your efforts align with your vision and prevent you from becoming overwhelmed by the sheer scope of what lies ahead.

The Importance of Prioritization

At the start of any journey, it's tempting to try to tackle everything at once. This approach, however, often leads to burnout, frustration, or failure to achieve meaningful results. Prioritization ensures that you focus on what matters most, maximizing your time and energy.

- Build Momentum: Starting with high-impact areas allows you to experience visible progress quickly, keeping you motivated to continue.
- Efficient Use of Resources: Concentrating on key areas ensures your time, energy, and money are directed toward tasks that will yield the greatest benefit.
- Reduce Overwhelm: Breaking down a large project into smaller, prioritized tasks makes it more manageable.
- Align Efforts with Goals: Prioritizing ensures that your actions are intentional and aligned with your broader vision.

By focusing on priority areas, you create a strong foundation for long-term success.

Steps to Identify High-Impact Areas

1. Define Your Ultimate Goals

Before identifying priority areas, take a step back and define what success looks like for you. For example:

- Is your goal to create a more peaceful and organized home?
- Are you striving to simplify your daily routines?
- Do you want to reclaim time by eliminating unnecessary tasks?

Understanding your end goal will guide you in selecting areas that align with your vision.

2. Assess Your Current Situation

Take a close look at your environment or circumstances. Identifying pain points will help you determine which areas need immediate attention. For example:

- Which areas of your home or life feel the most chaotic or unmanageable?
- Are there specific spaces or habits that create stress or inefficiency?
- What tasks or areas consume the most time or energy without adding value?

For instance, if your cluttered entryway causes daily frustration as you scramble to find your keys, this could be a high-impact area to prioritize.

3. Evaluate the Impact of Change

Not all areas are created equal when it comes to the impact of improvement. Ask yourself:

- Which areas will have the most immediate and visible effect if improved?
- Are there any areas that will provide long-term benefits once addressed?
- Will fixing this area make it easier to tackle other tasks or goals?

For example, organizing your kitchen can streamline daily meal prep and reduce stress, making it a high-impact starting point. On the other hand, decluttering an unused attic may have less immediate impact on your day-to-day life.

4. Consider Emotional and Practical Significance

Some areas carry emotional weight, while others may be purely practical. Prioritize spaces or tasks that evoke strong feelings or contribute significantly to your well-being. For example:

- Sentimental clutter in your bedroom may weigh on you emotionally, making it a high-priority area to address.
- Clearing out your workspace may improve focus and productivity, offering practical benefits.

Balancing emotional and practical priorities ensures a holistic approach.

5. Start Small, Think Big

While it's important to think about the big picture, starting with smaller, manageable tasks can help build momentum. For example, rather than tackling an entire room, focus on a single drawer, shelf, or section. These small wins will encourage you to continue and give you a sense of accomplishment early on.

Common High-Impact Areas to Focus On

While every person's priorities will vary, certain areas tend to have a universally high impact when improved. Here are a few examples:

1. Entryway

The entryway is the first thing you see when you come home and the last thing you see when you leave. A clutter-free entryway can set a positive tone for the day and reduce stress. Focus on:

- Organizing shoes, coats, and bags.
- Adding hooks or shelves for keys and essentials.
- Creating a designated space for mail and other items.

2. Kitchen

The kitchen is often the heart of the home, and an organized kitchen can make daily tasks like cooking and meal prep more efficient. High-impact changes might include:

- Decluttering countertops.
- Organizing pantry shelves and discarding expired items.
- Creating designated zones for utensils, pots, and appliances.

3. Bedroom

A clutter-free bedroom promotes relaxation and better sleep, making it a high-priority area for many people. Focus on:

- Clearing surfaces like nightstands and dressers.

- Organizing closets and drawers.
- Removing items that don't belong in the bedroom, like work-related materials or unused furniture.

4. Workspace

If you work from home or have a dedicated workspace, keeping it organized can boost productivity and reduce distractions. Consider:

- Decluttering your desk and filing important documents.
- Managing cables and cords.
- Creating a system for organizing supplies.

5. Living Room

As a shared space, the living room can quickly become cluttered. Addressing this area can improve comfort and functionality for everyone in your household. Focus on:

- Organizing shelves and surfaces.
- Minimizing excess decor and furniture.
- Creating designated storage for items like remote controls, blankets, and games.

Creating an Action Plan

Once you've identified your priority areas, it's time to create a focused action plan.

Step 1: List Your Priority Areas

Write down the areas you've identified as high impact. Rank them in order of importance or urgency.

Step 2: Break Down Tasks

Divide each priority area into smaller tasks. For example, if your priority is the kitchen, your task list might include:

- Empty and clean pantry shelves.
- Discard expired items.
- Group similar items together (e.g., snacks, spices, canned goods).
- Label containers and bins for easy access.

Step 3: Set Deadlines

Assign a deadline for each task to maintain momentum. Be realistic about how much time you can dedicate and adjust as needed.

Step 4: Gather Tools and Resources

Ensure you have everything you need before starting. This might include storage bins, labels, cleaning supplies, or donation bags.

Step 5: Take Action

Start with one area and complete it fully before moving on to the next. Avoid the temptation to jump between tasks, as this can create chaos and reduce efficiency.

Staying Focused and Motivated

- Visualize Success: Picture how your space will look and feel once the priority area is addressed.
- Celebrate Small Wins: Acknowledge and reward yourself for completing tasks, no matter how small.
- Ask for Help: Enlist the support of family or friends to make the process faster and more enjoyable.
- Reassess Priorities: As you progress, revisit your list to ensure your focus remains aligned with your goals.

Chapter 5: Building Your Decluttering Toolkit

Essential Supplies: Tools for Decluttering Success

Decluttering your home or workspace is a transformative process, but like any project, having the right tools makes all the difference. When it comes to clearing clutter, essential supplies such as boxes, labels, and storage solutions are your trusted allies. They streamline the process, enhance organization, and ensure long-term success.

Boxes: The Backbone of Decluttering

Boxes are among the most versatile and essential tools in any decluttering project. They help you sort, store, and transport items efficiently, making them a cornerstone of the organization process.

Different Types of Boxes

- Cardboard Boxes: Ideal for temporary sorting and donations, these are affordable and readily available. They are perfect for categorizing items during the decluttering process.

- Plastic Storage Bins: Durable and stackable, plastic bins are excellent for long-term storage. Opt for clear bins so you can see the contents at a glance.
- Decorative Boxes: For items you want to keep visible yet organized, decorative boxes add functionality and style to your space.

How to Use Boxes in Decluttering?

- The Four-Box Method: Use four labelled boxes— Keep, Donate, Toss, and Relocate. This method simplifies decision-making and helps you categorize items efficiently.
- Seasonal Storage: Use large, labelled boxes for seasonal items like holiday decorations, winter clothing, or summer gear. Store them in designated areas like the attic or garage.
- Temporary Holding: When working on larger spaces, use boxes to temporarily hold items while you clean or reorganize.

Tips for Maximizing Box Usage

- Label all boxes clearly to avoid confusion later.

- Avoid overfilling boxes to ensure they are easy to carry.
- Use smaller boxes for heavier items like books to prevent strain.

Labels: The Key to Clarity

Labels are the unsung heroes of decluttering. A clear, visible label prevents guesswork and ensures that every item finds its rightful place.

Types of Labels

- Pre-Made Stickers: These are available in stores and come with common categories like "Toys," "Books," or "Kitchen."
- Custom Labels: Create your own using label makers or printable sticker sheets. Customize them with specific categories or colour codes.
- Reusable Labels: Consider chalkboard or dry-erase labels for storage bins where contents may change over time.

How Labels Enhance Organization

- Immediate Identification: Labelled boxes and bins help you identify contents at a glance, saving time and effort.
- Consistency: When everything is labelled, it creates a sense of order and consistency in your space.
- Accountability: Labels make it easier for others in your household to maintain organization, as they clearly indicate where items belong.

Effective Labelling Tips

- Use large, legible fonts for easy readability.
- Include both text and icons for visual clarity, especially for children.
- Match labels to their corresponding category in your overall organization system.

Storage Solutions: Turning Chaos into Order

Storage solutions come in many forms, from shelves and bins to furniture with built-in storage. The right storage solutions are essential for maintaining a clutter-free environment.

Choosing the Right Storage Solutions

- Shelves: Use wall-mounted or freestanding shelves to maximize vertical space. These are perfect for books, decorative items, or frequently used supplies.
- Drawer Organizers: Divide drawer space into sections for items like utensils, office supplies, or makeup.
- Under-Bed Storage: Utilize the space under your bed with flat bins for seasonal clothing or bedding.
- Multi-Functional Furniture: Invest in furniture with hidden storage, such as ottomans, coffee tables with compartments, or beds with built-in drawers.

Long-Term Benefits of Storage Solutions

- Space Optimization: Proper storage allows you to make the most of every inch of your home.
- Reduced Visual Clutter: Items tucked away in storage create a clean, calming environment.
- Accessibility: Well-organized storage ensures you can find what you need quickly and easily.

Tips for Using Storage Solutions

- Prioritize accessibility by storing frequently used items in easily reachable places.
- Use clear or transparent containers for items that you need to identify quickly.
- Regularly review your stored items to avoid unnecessary accumulation.

Combining Tools for Maximum Impact

The true power of decluttering tools lies in their combined use. Boxes, labels, and storage solutions work together to create a seamless system of organization.

Sorting with Boxes and Labels

During the decluttering process, use labeled boxes to categorize items. For example:

- A box labelled "Donate" for items you no longer need but can give away.
- A box labelled "Keep" for items you intend to store in their proper place.

Integrating Storage Solutions

Once you've sorted your items, transfer them into appropriate storage solutions.

- Seasonal clothing can go into labelled under-bed storage bins.
- Frequently accessed tools or supplies can be organized on labelled shelves.

Creating a System

- Assign a specific storage area for each category of items.
- Use consistent labelling and storage types for similar categories to create a cohesive look.

Additional Supplies to Enhance Your Decluttering Efforts

While boxes, labels, and storage solutions are the core tools, there are additional supplies that can further aid the process:

- Trash Bags: For items you plan to discard, sturdy trash bags are essential.
- Markers or Label Makers: These make creating labels quick and easy.
- Vacuum-Seal Bags: Great for compressing bulky items like blankets or seasonal clothing.

- Cleaning Supplies: A decluttered space often requires a thorough cleaning. Stock up on sprays, cloths, and dusters.
- Hooks and Hangers: For organizing closets and vertical spaces.

The Emotional Impact of Having the Right Tools

Decluttering can be an emotional journey, but having the right supplies can make it manageable and even enjoyable. Tools like boxes and labels provide structure, reducing overwhelm and helping you focus on one step at a time. Storage solutions give you a sense of control over your space, fostering a sense of accomplishment and peace.

Digital Organizing Tools: Apps and Systems to Streamline Files and Tasks

Digital clutter is as prevalent as physical clutter. From overflowing email inboxes to a chaotic assortment of files scattered across devices, digital disorganization can cause stress, hinder productivity, and reduce efficiency. Fortunately, digital organizing tools offer powerful solutions to streamline files and tasks, helping individuals and teams stay on top of their responsibilities while maintaining clarity in their digital spaces.

The Need for Digital Organization

Digital clutter accumulates rapidly due to constant information flow, from work documents and emails to photos and personal files. Without a structured approach, finding critical information becomes a daunting task. Digital organizing tools address this by:

- Boosting Productivity: Streamlined files and tasks lead to fewer distractions and more focus.
- Saving Time: Quickly locate important files or track project progress.
- Enhancing Collaboration: Teams can work seamlessly with shared tools.
- Reducing Stress: An organized digital environment fosters a sense of control and calmness.

Essential Digital Organizing Tools

1. File Management Tools

Effective file organization is the foundation of digital decluttering. File management tools help sort, store, and retrieve documents effortlessly.

Google Drive:

A cloud-based solution, Google Drive offers secure storage, real-time collaboration, and access to files from anywhere. Organize files into folders, subfolders, and categories for easy retrieval.

- Features: File sharing, integration with Google Docs/Sheets, advanced search functionality.
- Best for: Individuals and teams needing collaborative file storage.

Dropbox:

Known for its user-friendly interface, Dropbox provides cloud storage for organizing and syncing files across devices.

- Features: File version history, offline access, and third-party app integrations.

- Best for: Professionals seeking simple yet robust file storage.

OneDrive:

Microsoft's cloud service integrates seamlessly with Office tools like Word, Excel, and PowerPoint.

- Features: Automatic syncing with Windows devices, file-sharing links, and large storage plans.
- Best for: Users in the Microsoft ecosystem.

2. Task Management Tools

Keeping track of tasks and deadlines is essential for productivity. Task management tools streamline workflows by providing clear overviews of priorities and progress.

Trello:

Trello uses a Kanban-style board system to organize tasks visually. It's great for individuals and teams to manage projects at a glance.

- Features: Customizable boards, drag-and-drop cards, and task deadlines.
- Best for: Visual learners and collaborative teams.

Asana:

Asana is a robust tool that offers task management for complex projects. Users can track milestones, assign tasks, and monitor progress efficiently.

- Features: Timeline views, project templates, and integration with other apps.
- Best for: Businesses handling multi-phase projects.

Todoist:

A minimalist app that helps users manage daily to-do lists, set reminders, and organize tasks by priority.

- Features: Task categorization, recurring reminders, and productivity tracking.
- Best for: Individuals seeking simplicity in task management.

3. Email Management Tools

An overflowing inbox can lead to missed opportunities and unnecessary stress. Email management tools help declutter and prioritize communication.

Microsoft Outlook:

A comprehensive tool for managing emails, calendars, and tasks in one place.

- Features: Focused Inbox for important emails, scheduling options, and integration with Microsoft apps.
- Best for: Professionals using the Microsoft Office suite.

Spark:

Spark organizes emails by priority and promotes collaboration through shared drafts and team inboxes.

- Features: Smart inbox, email snoozing, and collaborative email threads.
- Best for: Teams needing shared email management.

Clean Email:

Clean Email helps declutter your inbox by grouping emails into categories like subscriptions or social notifications, making mass deletion or organization simple.

- Features: Bulk actions, unsubscribe options, and automated filters.
- Best for: Those overwhelmed by email overload.

4. Note-Taking and Knowledge Management Tools

Organizing ideas, notes, and important information is essential for personal and professional growth.

Evernote:

A popular tool for capturing notes, creating to-do lists, and saving web clippings.

- Features: Searchable tags, voice note capability, and device syncing.
- Best for: Individuals managing extensive notes and ideas.

Notion:

Notion combines note-taking, task management, and collaboration into one platform. Users can build custom databases to organize information.

- Features: Templates, integration with other apps, and a drag-and-drop interface.
- Best for: Creative professionals and teams needing a flexible workspace.

Microsoft OneNote:

A digital notebook tool perfect for capturing ideas, drawings, or meeting notes.

- Features: Section-based organization, handwriting recognition, and integration with Office apps.
- Best for: Students and professionals in the Microsoft ecosystem.

5. Password Management Tools

Managing multiple passwords securely is crucial in a digital world. Password management tools simplify this task while ensuring security.

Last Pass:

Stores passwords securely and autofill's login credentials for various websites.

- Features: Encrypted vault, password sharing, and multi-device syncing.
- Best for: Individuals and families managing multiple accounts.

Dash lane:

Offers password management along with dark web monitoring and VPN services.

- Features: Autofill, password health reports, and advanced security.
- Best for: Those prioritizing both password and internet security.

1Password:

Provides secure storage for passwords, documents, and sensitive information.

- Features: Family and team plans, travel mode, and biometric authentication.
- Best for: Users seeking a comprehensive security solution.

6. Digital Calendar and Scheduling Tools

Efficient time management is key to productivity, and digital calendars simplify planning.

Google Calendar:

A user-friendly tool for scheduling appointments, events, and reminders.

- Features: Sync across devices, shared calendars, and color-coded events.
- Best for: Individuals and teams needing accessible scheduling.

Microsoft Calendar:

Integrated into Outlook, this tool provides seamless scheduling alongside email and task management.

- Features: Shared availability, recurring events, and group scheduling.
- Best for: Teams using Microsoft Office.

How to Choose the Right Tools?

With so many options, selecting the best tools depends on your unique needs. Consider the following:

- Compatibility: Ensure the tool works seamlessly with your existing devices and software.
- Usability: Opt for tools with intuitive interfaces and minimal learning curves.
- Scalability: Choose tools that grow with your needs, whether for personal use or team collaboration.

- Budget: While some tools are free, premium versions often offer enhanced features.

Tips for Effective Digital Organization

- Set Aside Time: Dedicate regular intervals to clean up files, emails, and tasks.
- Use Automation: Leverage features like filters, auto-organization, and recurring reminders.
- Maintain Consistency: Stick to a standardized naming and folder system.
- Evaluate Periodically: Assess tools and workflows to ensure they remain effective.

Support Systems: How to Involve Family, Friends, or Professionals for Encouragement

Decluttering, whether it involves physical spaces, digital files, or mental load, can be a daunting process. While personal determination plays a significant role in achieving a clutter-free life, the journey becomes more manageable—and often more enjoyable—with the help of a strong support system. Family, friends, and professionals can provide encouragement, accountability, and practical assistance to help you stay motivated and on track.

The Importance of Support in Decluttering

The process of decluttering often stirs up emotional and psychological challenges. Sentimental attachments, decision fatigue, or fear of letting go can make it difficult to move forward. A support system provides:

- Emotional Encouragement: Offering reassurance during tough decisions.
- Motivational Boosts: Keeping you focused when you feel overwhelmed.
- Objective Perspectives: Helping you see items or habits in a new light.
- Practical Help: Assisting with sorting, organizing, or heavy lifting.

Involving Family in the Decluttering Process

Family members are often the closest and most readily available source of support. However, involving them effectively requires open communication and a collaborative approach.

1. Foster Open Dialogue

Start by explaining why you're embarking on a decluttering journey and how it aligns with shared family goals, such as reducing stress, creating more functional spaces, or improving quality of life. Encourage family members to share their thoughts and concerns to ensure everyone feels included.

2. Set Clear Boundaries

While family involvement is beneficial, it's important to establish boundaries. For example, let them know which areas or items you'd like to manage yourself and where you'd appreciate their help. This prevents misunderstandings and ensures your personal goals remain the priority.

3. Make It a Team Effort

Involving the entire family in decluttering sessions can foster a sense of unity and shared purpose. Consider assigning specific tasks based on individual strengths or preferences, such as:

- Sorting through old toys (kids).

- Organizing garage tools (spouse/partner).
- Scanning and digitizing family photos (tech-savvy members).

4. Turn It into a Fun Activity

Transform decluttering into a family event by adding an element of fun. Play upbeat music, turn it into a timed challenge, or celebrate milestones with a small reward like a family movie night.

Involving Friends as Supportive Allies

Friends can provide valuable perspectives and encouragement, especially when you're tackling sentimental or overwhelming clutter.

1. Choose the Right Friends

Select friends who understand and respect your goals. Ideally, they should be supportive, non-judgmental, and willing to help without imposing their own opinions.

2. Host Decluttering Parties

Invite friends to join you for a decluttering session. Offer snacks, make it social, and assign them roles such as:

- Helping sort items into keep/donate/discard piles.
- Offering a fresh perspective on sentimental items.
- Assisting with transportation for donations or recycling.

3. Use Friends for Accountability

Ask a close friend to be your accountability partner. Share your goals and progress with them, and schedule regular check-ins. Knowing someone is rooting for you can boost motivation and prevent procrastination.

4. Offer Reciprocity

Support is a two-way street. If a friend helps you with your decluttering, offer to return the favour by assisting them with their own organizational projects.

When to Seek Professional Help

While family and friends provide emotional and practical support, there are times when professional assistance is invaluable. Professionals bring expertise, objectivity, and efficiency to the decluttering process, helping you achieve results more quickly and effectively.

1. Professional Organizers

Hiring a professional organizer can transform your decluttering journey. These experts specialize in creating functional, sustainable systems tailored to your needs.

What They Do:

- Assess your spaces and identify problem areas.
- Provide strategies for sorting, purging, and organizing.
- Offer advice on storage solutions and maintenance habits.

Benefits:

- Expertise in tackling challenging spaces or items.
- Objective advice without emotional bias.
- Time-saving and stress-reducing approaches.

2. Therapists or Counsellors

For individuals struggling with deep emotional attachments or mental barriers to decluttering, a therapist or counsellor can provide critical support.

When to Consider Therapy:

- Difficulty letting go of sentimental items.
- Anxiety or guilt associated with decluttering.
- Compulsive hoarding tendencies.

Benefits:

- Identifying underlying emotional triggers.
- Developing healthier coping mechanisms.
- Gaining clarity and confidence to move forward.

3. Junk Removal Services

For large-scale decluttering projects or when dealing with heavy or bulky items, junk removal services can be a practical solution.

Services Offered:

- Removal of unwanted furniture, appliances, or debris.
- Recycling or donating items where possible.

Benefits:

- Saves time and effort.
- Eco-friendly disposal options.

4. Cleaning Services

Once clutter is cleared, professional cleaners can help refresh and sanitize your spaces, giving you a clean slate to maintain your newly organized environment.

Practical Tips for Leveraging Support Systems

1. Clearly Define Your Goals

Before seeking support, clarify your goals and vision. Share these with your support system to ensure everyone understands the desired outcome.

2. Be Open to Suggestions

While your goals are the priority, family, friends, or professionals may offer valuable ideas or perspectives. Stay open to constructive feedback.

3. Celebrate Milestones Together

Acknowledging and celebrating progress, whether it's decluttering a single room or completing an entire project, fosters positivity and motivation.

4. Practice Gratitude

Expressing gratitude strengthens relationships and ensures your support system feels appreciated. A heartfelt thank-you note, a small gift, or simply acknowledging their efforts can go a long way.

The Emotional Rewards of a Support System

Decluttering often extends beyond physical spaces, impacting mental clarity, emotional well-being, and relationships. Engaging a support system adds deeper dimensions to the process:

- Strengthened Bonds: Collaborating on a shared goal brings families and friends closer.
- Sense of Accomplishment: Achieving milestones with support fosters confidence and pride.
- Empowered Independence: With guidance from professionals, individuals gain skills to maintain order independently.

Chapter 6: Developing a Decluttering Strategy

The 5-Step Decluttering Method: Sort, Purge, Organize, Optimize, Maintain

Decluttering can often feel like an overwhelming task, but breaking it down into a structured, manageable process makes it not only achievable but also sustainable. The 5-Step Decluttering Method—Sort, Purge, Organize, Optimize, and Maintain—provides a clear roadmap to tackle clutter in every area of your life, whether it's physical, digital, or mental. Each step is designed to build upon the previous one, leading to a clutter-free environment and a more productive, peaceful mindset.

Step 1: Sort – Categorizing What You Have

The first step in decluttering is sorting. This involves taking inventory of your belongings, categorizing them, and gaining clarity on what you own. Sorting helps you understand the scope of the clutter and lays the foundation for making informed decisions in the following steps.

How to Sort

- Group Similar Items Together: Start by gathering all similar items in one space. For example, if you're decluttering your closet, pull out all your clothes and place them on your bed. If you're working on your digital files, group documents, photos, and emails into separate folders.
- Create Subcategories: Within each group, create subcategories to refine your organization. For clothing, you might sort items into shirts, pants, shoes, and accessories. For digital files, you could separate work documents from personal ones.
- Label or Identify: Use sticky notes, temporary labels, or digital tags to clearly identify each category. This will help you stay organized as you move to the next step.

Why Sorting Matters

Sorting provides a visual representation of the clutter, which often serves as a wake-up call. It also ensures you don't overlook items during the decluttering process. By categorizing everything first, you make the next step—purging—much more efficient.

Step 2: Purge – Letting Go of What You Don't Need

Purging is the heart of the decluttering process. This step involves making decisions about what to keep and what to let go of. It's where you confront emotional attachments, overcome decision fatigue, and create space for what truly matters.

How to Purge

Ask Key Questions: For each item, ask yourself:

- Do I use this regularly?
- Does this add value to my life?
- Would I buy this again if I didn't already own it?
- Does this bring me joy or serve a meaningful purpose?

Use the Four-Box Method: Have four boxes or bags labelled Keep, Donate, Recycle, and Trash. As you go through each category, place items in the appropriate box.

Be Honest and Realistic: Avoid the temptation to keep items "just in case." If something hasn't been used in the past year or doesn't align with your current lifestyle, it's likely time to let it go.

Overcoming Emotional Resistance

- Sentimental Items: Take photos of sentimental items you want to let go of. This preserves the memory without keeping the physical clutter.
- Guilt Purchases: Let go of items you bought but never used. Remember that keeping them won't bring back the money spent, but freeing up space will bring you peace.

Why Purging Matters

Purging eliminates the excess that clutters your space and mind. It allows you to focus on the items that truly matter and sets the stage for effective organization in the next step.

Step 3: Organize – Creating a System That Works for You

Once you've sorted and purged your belongings, it's time to organize what remains. This step is about giving everything a designated place and creating a system that makes it easy to find and use your items.

How to Organize

- Designate a Home for Everything: Assign a specific spot for each item, whether it's a drawer, shelf, or digital folder. This reduces the likelihood of items ending up out of place.

- Use Storage Solutions: Invest in storage tools like bins, baskets, drawer dividers, and file organizers. These tools help contain items and keep your space neat.

- Label Clearly: Use labels to identify the contents of bins, boxes, and folders. In the digital realm, create a consistent naming convention for files and folders.

- Prioritize Accessibility: Place frequently used items in easy-to-reach locations, while less frequently used items can be stored in less accessible areas.

Why Organizing Matters

A well-organized space saves time, reduces stress, and enhances productivity. When everything has a designated place, you're less likely to waste time searching for items or feel overwhelmed by disorganization.

Step 4: Optimize – Streamlining for Efficiency

Optimization takes organization to the next level by streamlining systems for greater efficiency and convenience. This step ensures that your space and processes work seamlessly to support your daily life.

How to Optimize

- Simplify Processes: Look for ways to simplify how you access and use your items. For example, in the kitchen, group commonly used tools and ingredients together for easy meal preparation.
- Embrace Minimalism: Consider whether you can reduce the number of items even further. The fewer items you have, the easier it is to maintain an organized space.
- Invest in Multifunctional Tools: Choose items that serve multiple purposes to reduce clutter. For example, a bed with built-in storage or a digital device that consolidates multiple functions.
- Digital Automation: For digital clutter, automate repetitive tasks like file backups, email sorting, or calendar reminders.

Why Optimizing Matters

Optimization saves time and energy by ensuring that your space and systems are designed for maximum efficiency. It eliminates unnecessary steps and makes it easier to maintain the results of your decluttering efforts.

Step 5: Maintain – Sustaining a Clutter-Free Life

The final step is maintenance. Decluttering is not a one-time event but an ongoing practice. By developing habits and routines to keep clutter at bay, you can sustain the benefits of your efforts over the long term.

How to Maintain

- Adopt the One-In, One-Out Rule: For every new item you bring into your space, commit to letting go of an existing item. This prevents accumulation and keeps your belongings in balance.
- Regular Decluttering Sessions: Schedule periodic decluttering sessions to reassess your belongings and make adjustments as needed. This could be monthly, seasonally, or annually.
- Daily Tidying Habits: Spend a few minutes each day tidying up. Return items to their designated

places, clear surfaces, and address minor messes before they escalate.

- Mindful Consumption: Before making new purchases, pause to consider whether the item is truly necessary and aligns with your values and goals.
- Digital Hygiene: Regularly delete unnecessary files, unsubscribe from emails, and clean up your devices to prevent digital clutter from building up.

Why Maintaining Matters

Without maintenance, clutter will inevitably creep back into your life. By establishing simple, sustainable habits, you can preserve the results of your decluttering efforts and enjoy a consistently organized and peaceful environment.

Practical Systems: The Four-Box Method and the "One-In-One-Out" Rule

Decluttering is as much about having a plan as it is about execution. Without practical systems in place, even the best intentions can falter. Two simple yet highly effective systems—the Four-Box Method and the "One-In-One-

Out" Rule—are foundational tools that help organize the process and maintain a clutter-free environment.

The Four-Box Method

The Four-Box Method is a straightforward system for decluttering any space. It involves categorizing items into four boxes or piles labelled **Keep**, **Donate**, **Recycle**, and **Trash**. This method simplifies decision-making, eliminates ambiguity, and helps you systematically work through your clutter.

How the Four-Box Method Works

Gather Your Supplies:

Start by getting four boxes, bins, or bags. Clearly label them with the categories:

- Keep: Items you use regularly, value deeply, or genuinely need.
- Donate: Items in good condition that no longer serve you but could benefit someone else.
- Recycle: Items that are no longer usable but can be recycled, such as paper, glass, or electronics.
- Trash: Items that are damaged, expired, or unusable and cannot be donated or recycled.

Choose a Space:

Pick one area to focus on—such as a drawer, a shelf, or a closet. By working in small, defined sections, you avoid feeling overwhelmed and build momentum as you progress.

Handle Each Item Once:

Take each item in the space and place it into one of the four boxes. Avoid putting items back into the area without making a deliberate decision.

Process Each Box:

- For Keep items, return them to their designated places.
- For Donate items, take them to a local charity or arrange for pickup.
- For Recycle items, find the appropriate recycling facility or drop-off location.
- For Trash items, dispose of them responsibly, especially if they require special handling, like batteries or electronics.

Benefits of the Four-Box Method

- Simplicity: The method is easy to follow and adaptable to any type of clutter—physical, digital, or even mental.
- Accountability: By categorizing every item, you're forced to confront the true value or usefulness of each possession.
- Action-Oriented: The system provides clear next steps for each category, reducing procrastination.

Adapting the Method for Digital Clutter

The Four-Box Method can also be applied to digital clutter. For example:

- Keep: Files and emails you need to access regularly.
- Donate: Shareable resources or tools that can benefit others (e.g., forwarding helpful documents).
- Recycle: Outdated files that can be archived or stored externally.
- Trash: Unnecessary files, duplicate photos, or spam emails.

The "One-In-One-Out" Rule

While the Four-Box Method is excellent for the decluttering process, the "One-In-One-Out" Rule is a maintenance tool designed to prevent future clutter from accumulating.

What Is the One-In-One-Out Rule?

The rule is simple: For every new item you bring into your space, you must remove an existing item of equal size, category, or function. This creates a balance and ensures that your possessions remain manageable over time.

How to Implement the Rule?

- Set Clear Boundaries: Decide which areas of your life the rule will apply to. For example, you might use it for clothing, kitchen tools, or digital apps.
- Establish a Habit: Make it a routine to assess what to let go of every time you acquire something new. For instance, when you buy a new pair of shoes, identify an old pair to donate or discard.
- Be Honest and Consistent: Stick to the rule, even if it feels inconvenient at times. The goal is to

maintain equilibrium and avoid falling back into old habits.

Benefits of the One-In-One-Out Rule

- Prevention of Over accumulation: The rule helps you maintain the decluttered state you worked hard to achieve.
- Mindful Consumption: It encourages you to think twice before making new purchases, as you'll need to part with something in return.
- Sustainability: By donating or recycling items you no longer need, you contribute to reducing waste and supporting others.

Tips for Digital Application

The One-In-One-Out Rule can also be applied to your digital life:

- When you download a new app, delete one you no longer use.
- For every new digital subscription, cancel one that's redundant.
- Replace outdated files with updated versions to avoid duplication.

Scheduling Sessions: Carving Out Time for Regular Decluttering Efforts

Decluttering isn't a one-time event—it's an ongoing process that requires regular attention. Scheduling dedicated sessions ensures you stay on top of clutter and prevents it from building up again.

Why Schedule Decluttering Sessions?

- Consistency Creates Habits: Regularly setting aside time for decluttering helps you establish a habit, making it a natural part of your routine.
- Prevents Overwhelm: By tackling clutter in small, manageable increments, you avoid feeling overwhelmed by the scope of the task.
- Maintains Results: Scheduled sessions ensure your space remains organized and functional over time.

How to Schedule Decluttering Sessions?

1. Start Small

If the idea of dedicating a full day to decluttering feels daunting, start with short, focused sessions. Even 15–30 minutes a day can make a significant impact over time.

2. Set Realistic Goals

Determine what you want to accomplish during each session. For example, you might focus on decluttering a single drawer, your inbox, or a specific shelf. Setting achievable goals helps you measure progress and stay motivated.

3. Choose a Regular Time

Find a time that works best for your schedule and stick to it. This could be a weekly Saturday morning session, a daily 15-minute evening routine, or a monthly deep-cleaning day.

4. Use Timers for Focus

Set a timer to stay focused and avoid getting side-tracked. A popular method is the Pomodoro Technique— work for 25 minutes, take a 5-minute break, and repeat.

5. Make It Enjoyable

Turn decluttering into an enjoyable activity by playing music, listening to a podcast, or involving family members. Associating positive emotions with decluttering makes it easier to commit to regular sessions.

Creating a Decluttering Calendar

For larger decluttering projects, consider creating a calendar to organize your efforts:

- Daily: Spend 10–15 minutes tidying up surfaces and returning items to their designated places.
- Weekly: Dedicate an hour to decluttering a specific area, such as your closet, pantry, or desk.
- Monthly: Choose a larger project, such as deep-cleaning your garage or organizing digital photos.
- Seasonally: Declutter areas that naturally accumulate clutter over time, like holiday decorations, seasonal clothing, or outdoor equipment.

Benefits of Scheduling Decluttering Sessions

- Reduces Decision Fatigue: By setting a schedule in advance, you eliminate the need to decide when and where to declutter.
- Builds Momentum: Regular sessions create a sense of accomplishment and build momentum for larger projects.

- Supports Long-Term Change: Scheduling ensures that decluttering becomes a sustainable habit, rather than a sporadic effort.

Combining Practical Systems and Scheduling for Long-Term Success

The combination of practical systems like the Four-Box Method and the "One-In-One-Out" Rule, along with scheduled decluttering sessions, creates a powerful framework for achieving and maintaining a clutter-free life.

- The Four-Box Method provides a structured way to tackle clutter and make decisions about your possessions.
- The One-In-One-Out Rule helps you prevent future clutter and encourages mindful consumption.
- Scheduling Sessions ensures consistency and keeps your space organized over time.

By incorporating these strategies into your life, you'll not only enjoy the benefits of a decluttered environment but also experience greater peace of mind, productivity, and overall well-being. The key is to start small, stay consistent, and embrace the process as a journey toward a more intentional and fulfilling lifestyle.

Chapter 7: Decluttering Your Home

Room-by-Room Guide: Organizing Your Home for Function and Serenity

Keeping a home organized isn't just about tidying up; it's about creating a living space where everything has its place, allowing for both function and peace of mind. An organized home fosters a sense of calm, productivity, and satisfaction, improving your overall quality of life. A room-by-room guide can provide structure to your efforts, turning what might feel like an overwhelming task into manageable steps. Whether you're moving into a new home, preparing for a life event, or simply seeking to declutter and refresh.

Entryway and Living Spaces

The entryway serves as the first impression of your home and is often the most cluttered area, given the shoes, coats, bags, and other items that tend to accumulate. It's essential to create a system that minimizes chaos while still providing easy access to items you use regularly.

- Step 1: Declutter Start by removing any items that don't belong in the entryway. Old shoes, unused coats, and excess bags can quickly take up space. Keep only what you use on a daily basis—such as a key rack, a mirror, and a small shoe rack or bench.

- Step 2: Functional Storage Solutions Install hooks or a coat rack to keep jackets, scarves, and bags off the floor. Use baskets or bins to store items like hats and gloves, and consider a small table or console for keys and mail. If space allows, a small bench can be a practical addition for sitting while putting on shoes.

- Step 3: Living Room Organization The living room is where you entertain, relax, and unwind, so it needs to be both functional and aesthetically pleasing. Start by removing any items that don't belong in the living room. Then, organize furniture for ease of movement and conversation flow. Use multi-functional furniture, such as storage ottomans, coffee tables with drawers, or side tables with hidden compartments, to maximize space.

- Step 4: Storage and Display Create storage solutions for media devices, books, and other personal items. Consider adding a media cabinet or shelving units that fit seamlessly into the space. For decor, keep it minimal yet personal—curate meaningful items like photos, plants, or artwork, but avoid overcrowding surfaces to keep the space serene and uncluttered.

Kitchen and Pantry

The kitchen is often the heart of the home, but it can also become one of the most cluttered rooms, with pots, pans, and pantry items everywhere. A well-organized kitchen makes cooking and cleaning much easier, ensuring that meal preparation is as efficient and stress-free as possible.

- Step 1: Purge Expired or Unused Items Go through your pantry, fridge, and cabinets, removing any items that are expired, unopened but unlikely to be used, or duplicates. Also, check under the sink for old cleaning products or supplies that have gone unused.
- Step 2: Organize Cabinets and Drawers Group similar items together: baking goods, canned goods, oils and vinegars, and snacks. Use clear storage bins or baskets for smaller items like spice jars or tea bags. Drawer dividers for

utensils, and cutlery trays can help create a system that makes it easier to find what you need when cooking.

- Step 3: Maximize Counter Space Counter space can become cluttered quickly with appliances, utensils, and dishes. To keep it clear, store bulky appliances like mixers or blenders in cabinets or on shelves when not in use. Keep only your most frequently used tools and appliances within easy reach, and clear off counters after every meal preparation.

- Step 4: Pantry Organization Use clear glass or plastic containers for dry goods like flour, rice, pasta, and cereals. Label them for easy identification. Install adjustable shelves or bins for canned goods and jars. Make sure to place older items at the front so that you use them first, minimizing waste and ensuring you don't miss out on expiration dates.

Bedroom and Closets

Your bedroom should be a sanctuary—a peaceful retreat where you rest and recharge. However, cluttered drawers and overflowing closets can cause unnecessary stress and disrupt relaxation. Let's break down an effective organization strategy for the bedroom and closet.

- Step 1: Declutter and Simplify Remove any items that don't belong in the bedroom, including work papers, laundry, or other clutter that may make the space feel chaotic. Only keep what's necessary or meaningful, such as comfortable bedding, personal items, or a few decorative pieces.

- Step 2: Organize Closets Start by categorizing your clothing into categories such as work, casual, seasonal, and formal wear. Use matching hangers to create a uniform look and install hooks or a shoe rack to keep accessories and footwear tidy. Consider drawer dividers for smaller items like socks, scarves, or lingerie. If your closet is small, use under-bed storage for off-season clothing or extra bedding.

- Step 3: Maximize Storage Space Use the space under the bed for storage bins or boxes to keep extra items organized and out of sight

Bathroom

The bathroom is often a small space that needs to serve multiple functions—getting ready in the morning, unwinding after a long day, and storing all sorts of products. Effective organization in the bathroom is all about maximizing space while maintaining easy access to toiletries.

- Step 1: Declutter Surfaces and Cabinets Begin by clearing off countertops, removing old or expired products, and organizing your medicine cabinet. Remove anything from the bathroom that you don't use regularly or that has exceeded its shelf life.
- Step 2: Organize Toiletries and Products Use baskets or drawer dividers to separate toiletries, such as hair products, lotions, and cosmetics. A small tray can help organize frequently used items like soap, toothpaste, and a toothbrush holder. For makeup, consider drawer organizers or acrylic containers to keep everything easily visible and accessible.
- Step 3: Optimize Storage Space Make use of vertical space with shelves or wall-mounted

organizers to store towels, extra toilet paper, or cleaning products. Use under-sink storage to store items like cleaning supplies or extra toiletries in bins or baskets. Consider using clear containers for easier identification of items and to maintain a tidy, functional space.

Garage and Storage Areas

The garage and storage areas of a home are often the catch-all spaces for seasonal items, tools, and sports equipment, making them prone to disorganization. Creating an efficient storage system in these spaces ensures that you have room for what you need and can easily access items when necessary.

- Step 1: Sort and Purge Go through everything in the garage or storage area, sorting items into categories—tools, holiday decorations, gardening supplies, sports gear, etc. Discard anything that is broken, unused, or no longer needed.
- Step 2: Create Zones for Different Categories Use shelving, hooks, pegboards, and storage bins to create specific zones for each category. Keep tools within reach, and use labelled boxes or bins for smaller items like nails, screws, and light bulbs.

Install overhead storage racks for seasonal items, and use stackable bins for less frequently accessed items.

- Step 3: Utilize Vertical and Overhead Space Take advantage of the vertical space by using wall-mounted shelves or pegboards to store tools, bikes, and other equipment. Overhead storage racks are great for storing seasonal decorations, luggage, or large containers that don't need to be accessed frequently.

Handling Special Challenges: Tackling Sentimental Items, Gifts, and Hobbies

Organizing a home isn't just about decluttering; it also involves dealing with the emotional attachment to certain items. Some things are more than just objects; they are memories, gifts, or hobbies that carry deep personal meaning. Dealing with sentimental items, gifts, and collections can be one of the most challenging parts of home organization. The emotional attachment can make it difficult to let go, leading to cluttered spaces and a sense of overwhelm.

However, organizing sentimental items doesn't have to mean throwing them away or disregarding their significance. It's about finding ways to respect their emotional value while creating a space that allows you to live comfortably and efficiently. Below are practical strategies for handling sentimental items, gifts, and hobbies, with a focus on maintaining emotional well-being while organizing.

1. Handling Sentimental Items

Sentimental items are often the hardest to part with, as they carry memories of significant life events or people. These could include things like childhood toys, family heirlooms, old letters, photographs, or even souvenirs from travel.

- Step 1: Acknowledge the Emotions Before diving into organizing sentimental items, take a moment to acknowledge the emotions that come with them. It's okay to feel nostalgic or sentimental. Give yourself permission to experience the feelings that arise but also remind yourself that the goal is to preserve the memories in a way that honours them without overcrowding your space.
- Step 2: Sort and Categorize Start by grouping your sentimental items into categories. For example, you might have a category for family heirlooms,

one for childhood memorabilia, and another for items related to special events or vacations. Organizing them by theme can help you make sense of your collection and allow you to assess the importance of each item. It also provides a clearer picture of what you actually have.

- Step 3: Reflect on the Importance Go through each item and consider its emotional value. Ask yourself whether it still holds the same significance as it once did. Is the item truly something that you still cherish, or is it something you're holding on to out of guilt or obligation? If it no longer serves a purpose in your life, it may be time to let go. But if it still brings you joy or holds significant meaning, it might be worth keeping.

- Step 4: Create Memory Boxes or Albums One of the most effective ways to store sentimental items while saving space is to create memory boxes or albums. This approach allows you to preserve the items without them taking over your home. Use clear plastic bins or decorative boxes to store items like letters, photographs, or small mementos. For larger items, consider creating a dedicated memory album with photos of objects or people, adding context or personal stories alongside them.

- Step 5: Display Select Items Instead of keeping all sentimental items hidden away, consider displaying a select few that hold the most significance to you. A cherished family heirloom can be showcased in a glass cabinet, or a framed photograph from a meaningful event can serve as decor. By curating your collection, you can keep the emotional connection alive while maintaining an organized space.

- Step 6: Digitize When Possible for items like old photographs, letters, or documents, consider scanning or photographing them to create digital copies. This allows you to preserve the memory without taking up physical space. There are various services and apps that can help you organize and store digital files, making them accessible whenever you want to revisit them.

2. Handling Gifts

Gifts are another category of items that can lead to clutter and disorganization. Often, we receive gifts out of love and appreciation, but sometimes we're left with items that don't suit our style or that we simply don't need. The emotional challenge here is that getting rid of a gift can feel disrespectful or ungrateful, even if we don't have room for it.

- Step 1: Appreciate the Gesture, Not the Object The first step in handling gifts is to appreciate the gesture behind the gift, rather than focusing on the object itself. Gifts are a form of love and thoughtfulness, and it's important to acknowledge the kindness of the giver. However, it's also essential to recognize that it's okay to release an item that no longer serves you or your space.

- Step 2: Set Boundaries for Gift Storage If you find yourself accumulating gifts, set boundaries for how much space you're willing to allocate to gift items. For example, you could designate a specific shelf or storage bin for gifts, and once that space is full, it's time to let go of something else. By establishing limits, you can control the flow of gifts into your home while still honouring the thoughtfulness of the giver.

- Step 3: Re-Gift or Donate If you receive a gift that you don't need or don't use, consider re-gifting it (with care) or donating it to a charity. Be sure to do this in a respectful manner, as you don't want to hurt anyone's feelings. If you decide to donate a gift, choose a cause that aligns with the gift's purpose. Many people appreciate the chance to pass on items they no longer need, and this can keep the gift's spirit alive by finding it a new home.

- Step 4: Repurpose or Reimagine If you feel conflicted about parting with a gift, think about how you could repurpose it. Can you turn a decorative item into something functional? For instance, a gift that doesn't match your aesthetic could be transformed with a new coat of paint or fabric, giving it a fresh life in your home. By doing so, you honour the gift while making it more aligned with your personal space.

- Step 5: Express Gratitude Lastly, always take the time to thank the person who gave you the gift, regardless of whether you keep the item. Expressing genuine gratitude will assure them that their gesture was appreciated, even if the gift itself doesn't remain in your home.

3. Handling Hobbies and Collections

Hobbies and collections can be a source of joy and personal expression, but they can also take up significant space in your home. From model trains and sports memorabilia to crafting supplies and art collections, organizing hobbies and collections requires careful consideration to strike a balance between passion and practicality.

- Step 1: Assess the Current State of Your Collection Start by evaluating the current state of your hobby or collection. Is it growing out of control, or are you at a place where you want to downsize? Take stock of what you truly value in the collection. Which pieces are the most meaningful, and which ones might be surplus or not contributing to your overall enjoyment?
- Step 2: Curate Your Collection Consider curating your collection. This means displaying or keeping only the most significant pieces, while either selling or donating the rest. For example, if you collect figurines or artwork, select your favourite

pieces and give away or store the items that no longer resonate with you. By curating, you can turn your collection into a more manageable and meaningful display.

- Step 3: Organize Materials and Tools If you have a hobby that requires tools or materials—such as painting, knitting, or woodworking—organize these items by function. Use clear bins, storage boxes, or labelled drawers to separate materials like paints, yarn, or woodworking supplies. A designated hobby area can help keep your materials easily accessible while also creating a sense of order in your home.

- Step 4: Create Display Space for collections or finished works that you want to display, create dedicated display areas. Shelves, shadow boxes, or glass cabinets can keep your collection safe while showcasing it in an organized manner. Be mindful of how much space you want to dedicate to your hobby, and avoid overcrowding by rotating items periodically to maintain visual appeal.

- Step 5: Revaluate Regularly Hobbies and collections can evolve over time, so it's important to revaluate your collection on a regular basis. Periodically assess whether new items are truly enhancing your collection or if they are just adding to the clutter. Regularly pruning and curating your collection will help keep it manageable and relevant to your interests.

Creating Functional Spaces: Tips for Sustainable Organization

Now that we've explored how to handle sentimental items, gifts, and hobbies, it's important to discuss creating functional spaces that are not only organized but also sustainable in the long term. Sustainable organization ensures that your home remains clutter-free, efficient, and adaptable to changing needs.

1. Use Multi-Functional Furniture

In smaller spaces, multi-functional furniture can be a game-changer. Consider furniture pieces that serve multiple purposes, such as a coffee table with built-in storage, a bed with drawers underneath, or an ottoman that doubles as a seating area. These pieces help maximize space while keeping items organized and out of sight.

2. Implement Smart Storage Solutions

Storage solutions like vertical shelving, under-bed storage, and over-the-door organizers make use of unused space, helping you store items efficiently. Modular storage systems can be adapted to meet your needs as they change, making them a long-term organizational solution.

3. Stay Committed to Regular Decluttering

A key to sustainable organization is committing to regular decluttering. Whether it's once a season or once a year, set aside time to go through your belongings and remove anything that no longer serves you. This prevents clutter from accumulating over time and helps maintain the functionality of your home.

4. Digitize Paperwork

Paperwork can quickly pile up, creating unnecessary clutter. Implement a system for organizing important documents digitally. Use cloud storage or digital filing systems to store receipts, contracts, and important papers. This not only saves physical space but also makes it easier to find documents when needed.

5. Maintain an Organized System

To keep your home organized long-term, establish and maintain a system for how things are stored and put away. Whether it's labeling bins, creating designated spaces for specific categories, or using color-coding for organization, having a system in place ensures that everything has its place and helps you maintain order effortlessly.

Chapter 8: Decluttering Your Workplace

Physical Workspace: Organizing Your Desk, Drawers, and Supplies

A well-organized physical workspace is the foundation of productivity, creativity, and mental clarity. Whether you work in a bustling office, a quiet home environment, or a shared cowering space, the state of your desk and surrounding area can directly influence how efficiently you tackle tasks, how focused you remain, and how motivated you feel throughout the day. Organizing your desk, drawers, and supplies doesn't just result in a tidy space—it creates a haven for productivity and helps reduce stress.

The Benefits of an Organized Workspace

Before diving into the "how," let's understand why organizing your physical workspace is so important:

- Increased Productivity: A clutter-free desk reduces distractions, allowing you to focus on your tasks without unnecessary interruptions.
- Mental Clarity: A tidy workspace can help declutter your mind. A chaotic environment often leads to scattered thinking, while an organized one fosters calmness and focus.
- Time-Saving: When your supplies and tools are systematically arranged, you spend less time searching for items and more time accomplishing tasks.
- Reduced Stress: A messy workspace can contribute to feelings of overwhelm. In contrast, a neat space creates a sense of control and order.

- Enhanced Creativity: Clearing physical clutter often clears mental clutter, creating space for innovative thinking and problem-solving.

Step 1: Organizing Your Desk

Your desk is the centrepiece of your workspace. It's where the majority of your work happens, so keeping it functional and organized is crucial.

Declutter First

Clear Everything: Remove everything from your desk—papers, stationery, gadgets, and decorations. Start with a clean slate.

Sort Items: Separate items into three categories:

- Essentials (things you use daily, like your computer, notebook, and pen)
- Frequently Used Items (items you use weekly, like a stapler or calculator)
- Rarely Used or Decorative Items (things you use occasionally or purely for aesthetic purposes).

Purge Unnecessary Items: Get rid of anything you don't need. Old papers, broken pens, and outdated supplies take up valuable space.

Create Zones on Your Desk

Divide your desk into functional zones:

- Primary Zone: Place essential items within arm's reach—your computer, phone, notepad, and pen.
- Secondary Zone: This is for frequently used items like a water bottle, stapler, or small file organizer.
- Decorative Zone: Limit decorations to one or two meaningful items, like a plant or a photo, to avoid clutter.

Manage Cables

Tangled cables can make even the cleanest desk feel messy. Use cable organizers, clips, or a cable management box to keep cords neatly arranged and out of sight. Consider using wireless devices where possible to reduce cable clutter.

Utilize Vertical Space

If your desk has limited surface area, make use of vertical space. Install shelves or use a monitor stand with built-in storage to elevate your screen while creating extra space underneath.

Step 2: Decluttering and Structuring Your Drawers

Desk drawers often become the catch-all for random items, from loose paperclips to forgotten snacks. Here's how to reclaim order:

Empty and Sort

- Take Everything Out: Dump the contents of each drawer onto a flat surface to see what you're working with.
- Categorize Items: Group similar items together, such as writing tools, office supplies, and personal items.
- Discard or Relocate: Throw away broken or outdated items and relocate non-work-related items (like makeup or junk food) to their proper places.

Use Drawer Organizers

Invest in drawer dividers or organizers to keep items separated and easy to find. For example:

- Use small compartments for pens, paperclips, and sticky notes.
- Designate a section for larger items like notebooks or chargers.

- Include a tray or container for personal items like keys or a phone charger.

Create a System

Organize drawers by function. For example:

- Top Drawer: Store everyday essentials, like pens, notepads, and highlighters.
- Middle Drawer: Reserve this for frequently used supplies, such as staplers, tape, or scissors.
- Bottom Drawer: Use this for bulkier items like binders, files, or a small organizer for personal belongings.

Label your drawers if necessary, especially if you have multiple storage compartments. This helps maintain order and makes it easier to find things quickly.

Step 3: Managing Supplies

Office supplies are vital for productivity, but they can quickly create clutter if not properly managed.

Perform a Supply Audit

Take inventory of your supplies to determine what you have, what you need, and what you can discard. Many people hold onto excessive amounts of supplies they never use, like stacks of sticky notes or half-used pens.

Centralize Storage

If you work in a larger office or shared space, create a centralized area for infrequently used supplies. This frees up desk and drawer space while still keeping items accessible when needed.

Implement a Rotation System

Only keep what you need for the week or month in your immediate workspace. Store extra supplies—like unopened printer paper or surplus pens—in a separate storage area. Replenish your supplies as needed.

Choose Multi-Purpose Tools

Opt for supplies that serve multiple functions to save space. For example, use a pen with multiple ink colours instead of separate pens, or a combination stapler and hole punch.

Additional Tips for Maintaining an Organized Workspace

Establish Daily Habits

- Clear Your Desk Daily: At the end of each day, spend 5–10 minutes tidying up your workspace. File away papers, return supplies to their designated spots, and wipe down your desk.
- Adopt the "One-In-One-Out" Rule: For every new item you bring into your workspace, remove one to maintain balance.
- Perform Weekly Deep Cleans: Dedicate time each week to review your workspace and reorganize as needed.

Digital and Physical Integration

Your physical workspace should complement your digital workspace. For example:

- Use a docking station to reduce the clutter of laptops, monitors, and other devices.
- Keep a single notebook or planner for physical note-taking instead of scattered loose papers.
- Sync your filing system between physical folders and digital storage for seamless organization.

Personalize Thoughtfully

Adding personal touches to your workspace can make it feel inviting and inspiring. However, moderation is key.

Limit personal items to a few meaningful pieces that bring joy or motivation without overwhelming the space.

Use Natural Light and Ergonomics

Position your desk near a source of natural light to boost mood and productivity. Ensure your chair, desk, and monitor are set up ergonomically to support long hours of work.

Digital Decluttering: Managing Email, Files, and Apps

Digital clutter can be just as overwhelming as physical mess, if not more so. With the sheer volume of emails, files, and apps we interact with daily, it's easy to feel buried under a mountain of data. Digital decluttering helps create a streamlined, functional virtual environment, reducing stress, improving efficiency, and boosting focus. Here's how you can tackle each area:

Emails

Managing emails effectively can save hours of time and alleviate the frustration of sifting through a crowded inbox.

Adopt the Inbox Zero Philosophy

- Aim to clear your inbox regularly, keeping only actionable or critical emails.
- Archive messages you don't need immediate access to and delete unnecessary ones.

Set Up Folders and Filters

- Use folders or labels to categorize emails into actionable items, references, or specific projects.
- Set up automated filters to sort incoming messages. For example, direct newsletters to a "Reading" folder and client communications to a "Priority" folder.

Unsubscribe Aggressively

- Reduce incoming email clutter by unsubscribing from newsletters or promotional emails you no longer read. Services like Unroll.me can help speed up this process.

Schedule Email Time

- Avoid the constant distraction of checking emails throughout the day. Instead, designate specific times to review and respond to emails.

Use Search Efficiently

- Learn to leverage search functions within your email platform by using keywords, dates, or sender filters to quickly locate important messages.

Files

A disorganized file system can hinder productivity and increase frustration. Create an intuitive structure for your digital files with these steps:

Declutter and Delete

- Dedicate time to comb through your files, deleting duplicates, outdated documents, and irrelevant materials.

Adopt a Consistent Folder System

- Use a clear, hierarchical folder structure. For instance:
- Main Folder: Work
- Subfolder: Projects
- Sub-subfolder: Project A
- Be specific and consistent with naming conventions to make finding files easier.

Leverage Cloud Storage

- Use services like Google Drive, Dropbox, or OneDrive to store and access files from anywhere. Sync these tools across devices for seamless organization.

Automate Backups

- Prevent data loss by setting up regular automatic backups to cloud services or external hard drives.

Regular Maintenance

- Schedule periodic reviews of your files to keep them organized and remove unnecessary content. A monthly or quarterly review works well.

Apps

Apps are meant to simplify tasks, but an overabundance can create chaos. Audit and organize them for better functionality:

Evaluate Your Apps

- Delete unused apps that clutter your devices and drain storage. If you haven't opened an app in six months, you likely don't need it.

Organize Your Home Screen

- Arrange frequently used apps on your home screen for easy access. Group similar apps into folders, such as "Productivity," "Entertainment," and "Finance."

Use Focused Tools

- Avoid redundant apps by choosing multi-functional ones. For example, an app like Notion can replace separate tools for note-taking, task management, and project tracking.

Manage Notifications

- Disable non-essential notifications to minimize distractions and reclaim focus.

Perform App Audits

- Review your app library regularly to ensure every app serves a clear purpose.

Time Management: Removing Inefficiencies from Your Calendar

Time is one of our most valuable resources. Mismanagement leads to stress, missed deadlines, and reduced productivity. By streamlining your calendar and eliminating inefficiencies, you can reclaim control over your schedule.

Audit Your Current Calendar

Track Your Time

- Spend a week tracking how you spend your time to identify patterns, time-wasting activities, or overly packed days.
- Tools like Toggl or RescueTime can help with this process.

Analyze Your Commitments

- Are all meetings necessary? Are there recurring events that no longer serve their purpose?

Decline, delegate, or consolidate activities where possible.

Batch Similar Tasks

Grouping similar tasks can improve efficiency by minimizing context-switching. For example:

- Set aside specific blocks of time for answering emails, returning phone calls, or planning projects.
- Schedule meetings back-to-back to avoid fragmented workdays.

Implement Time Blocking

Time blocking involves allocating specific periods on your calendar for focused work, meetings, and breaks. This method:

- Reduces decision fatigue about what to work on next.
- Creates boundaries around tasks to prevent overworking.
- Ensures important priorities are given dedicated attention.

Say "No" More Often

Protect your calendar by being selective about what you agree to. Politely decline invitations, tasks, or meetings that aren't aligned with your goals or priorities.

Set Aside Buffer Time

Overloading your calendar can leave you feeling rushed. Include buffer time between meetings or projects to recharge, prepare, or address unforeseen delays.

Use Calendar Tools Effectively

- Colour-code events to distinguish between personal, professional, and recurring tasks.
- Set reminders for deadlines or important events.
- Sync your calendar across devices to ensure accessibility.

Designing for Productivity: Ergonomic and Aesthetic Improvements

The physical design of your workspace directly impacts your productivity, comfort, and overall well-being. Optimizing ergonomics and aesthetics can make your work environment both functional and inspiring.

Ergonomic Improvements

Choose the Right Chair

195

- Invest in an ergonomic chair that supports your back, promotes good posture, and adjusts to your height.

Position Your Desk and Screen

- Ensure your desk is at elbow height and your screen is at eye level to avoid strain. Consider using a monitor stand or adjustable desk.

Keyboard and Mouse Placement

- Keep your keyboard and mouse at a comfortable distance to reduce wrist strain. Use a wrist rest if necessary.

Lighting

- Position your workspace near natural light to reduce eye strain and boost mood. Use task lighting, such as an adjustable desk lamp, for focused tasks.

Prevent Screen Fatigue

- Follow the 20-20-20 rule: Every 20 minutes, look at something 20 feet away for 20 seconds to reduce eye strain.

Aesthetic Enhancements

Declutter Your Workspace

- A clean, tidy space encourages focus. Keep your desktop free of unnecessary items and store supplies in designated places.

Incorporate Personal Touches

- Add a plant, artwork, or motivational quote to make the space feel inviting and uniquely yours.

Use Colour Psychology

- Choose calming or inspiring colours for your workspace. Blue promotes focus, green fosters calmness, and yellow boosts energy.

Optimize Layout

- Arrange your workspace to minimize distractions and maximize functionality. Ensure everything you need is within easy reach.

Minimize Noise

- Use noise-cancelling headphones, a white noise machine, or soundproofing materials to reduce auditory distractions.

Smart Additions for Productivity

- Standing Desk: Alternating between sitting and standing can improve energy and posture.
- Cable Management: Use cable organizers to keep wires neat and prevent tangling.
- Vision Boards: Create a small vision board with your goals to stay motivated.

Maintaining Momentum

Once you've decluttered digitally, optimized your calendar, and designed your workspace for productivity, the challenge becomes maintaining these improvements. Here's how:

Schedule Regular Maintenance

- Set aside time weekly or monthly to reassess and declutter your digital and physical spaces.

Adopt New Habits Gradually

- Focus on small, sustainable changes rather than overhauling everything at once.

Stay Flexible

- Adjust your systems and setups as your needs and priorities evolve.

Reflect on Progress

- Periodically review how your changes have impacted your productivity and well-being. Use this insight to refine your strategies.

Chapter 9: Maintaining a Clutter-Free Life

Daily Habits: Simple Routines to Keep Clutter at Bay

Clutter doesn't accumulate overnight—it's the result of habits, or a lack thereof, over time. Fortunately, the same principle works in reverse: maintaining a clutter-free environment is achievable by cultivating small, consistent daily habits. These simple routines don't just keep clutter at bay; they also promote mental clarity, reduce stress, and create a more peaceful, organized living space.

1. The "One-Minute Rule"

The "one-minute rule" is a simple yet transformative habit. If a task takes less than one minute to complete, do it immediately. This could be hanging up your coat when you come home, putting dirty dishes directly into the dishwasher, or tossing junk mail into the recycling bin.

Why It Works: Small tasks left undone can quickly snowball into overwhelming clutter. By addressing them right away, you prevent clutter from taking root and keep your space consistently tidy.

2. Make Your Bed Every Morning

While it might seem insignificant, making your bed sets a positive tone for the day. It's a quick task that instantly makes your bedroom look more organized and creates a sense of accomplishment.

How to Make It a Habit: Commit to making your bed as soon as you wake up. The more consistently you do it, the more automatic it will become.

Bonus Tip: Keep your bedding simple—fewer pillows and decorative elements mean less effort.

3. Declutter as You Go

Throughout the day, look for opportunities to declutter in real-time. For example:

- When cooking, put ingredients and utensils away as soon as you're done with them.
- When changing clothes, immediately hang up what you'll wear again and toss dirty items into the laundry basket.
- Before leaving a room, scan for items that don't belong and return them to their proper places.

Why It Works: This habit keeps clutter from accumulating and makes tidying up feel less overwhelming.

4. Follow the "One in, One Out" Rule

Whenever you bring something new into your home—whether it's clothing, kitchen gadgets, or books—commit to removing a similar item. For example, if you buy a new pair of shoes, donate or discard an old pair.

How to Make It a Habit: Create a dedicated space (e.g., a donation bin or bag) for items you're ready to part with. Each time you acquire something new, place the outgoing item in this space.

Why It Works: This rule prevents excess accumulation and encourages mindful consumption.

5. Tidy Up Before Bed

Set aside 5–10 minutes each evening to do a quick sweep of your living space. Focus on returning items to their rightful places, wiping down surfaces, and addressing any visible clutter.

Why It Works: Waking up to a tidy home is far more energizing than starting the day surrounded by yesterday's mess. This habit ensures you begin each day with a clean slate.

6. Handle Paperwork Immediately

Paper clutter, such as bills, receipts, and junk mail, is a common source of frustration. To prevent it from piling up, adopt a "touch it once" approach.

- Open mail as soon as you receive it and sort it into categories: recycle, file, or act on.
- Digitize important documents, such as receipts or statements, to reduce physical clutter.
- Use a filing system or inbox tray for items requiring action, and review it daily.

Why It Works: Staying on top of paperwork eliminates the stress of searching through piles later.

7. Do a Daily 10-Minute Decluttering Session

Set a timer for 10 minutes and focus on decluttering a specific area—your desk, a drawer, or a small section of your living room. The time limit keeps the task manageable and prevents it from feeling overwhelming.

Why It Works: This habit allows you to make consistent progress without dedicating hours to cleaning. Over time, these small efforts add up to significant results.

8. Empty the Dishwasher and Laundry Promptly

One of the quickest ways clutter builds up is when dishes and laundry aren't put away promptly. Make it a habit to empty the dishwasher and fold laundry as soon as it's done.

How to Make It a Habit: Incorporate these tasks into your routine. For example, empty the dishwasher while your morning coffee brews, or fold laundry while watching your favourite show.

Why It Works: Keeping these systems in motion prevents backlogs and ensures your space stays organized.

9. Create Drop Zones

Designate specific spaces for commonly used items, such as keys, wallets, and bags. This prevents them from being scattered throughout your home and makes them easier to find when needed.

Why It Works: A well-organized drop zone eliminates the stress of misplaced items and reduces clutter in high-traffic areas.

Bonus Tip: Use trays, hooks, or baskets to keep these zones tidy and visually appealing.

10. Practice Mindful Consumption

One of the most effective ways to prevent clutter is to stop it at the source. Before buying something new, ask yourself:

- Do I truly need this item?

- Do I have space for it?
- Will it add value to my life?

Why It Works: Mindful consumption ensures that everything you bring into your home has a purpose, reducing the likelihood of accumulating unnecessary items.

11. Encourage Household Participation

If you share your living space with others, make clutter management a team effort. Assign age-appropriate tasks to children, and establish shared responsibilities with partners or roommates.

How to Make It a Habit:

- Create a daily or weekly chore chart.
- Set clear expectations for each person's role in keeping the space tidy.
- Celebrate progress together to build motivation and accountability.

Why It Works: A collaborative approach prevents any one person from feeling overwhelmed and fosters a shared sense of ownership.

12. Keep Surfaces Clear

Flat surfaces like countertops, tables, and desks are magnets for clutter. Make it a daily goal to keep these areas as clear as possible.

How to Make It a Habit:

- Avoid leaving random items on surfaces.
- Use trays or containers to organize essentials, like remote controls or toiletries.

Why It Works: Clear surfaces create a sense of order and make your space feel more open and inviting.

13. Regularly Assess "Clutter Hotspots"

Certain areas, like entryways, coffee tables, or kitchen counters, tend to attract clutter. Identify these hotspots and develop a routine for addressing them daily.

Why It Works: Tackling clutter in these areas prevents it from spreading to the rest of your home.

14. Stay Consistent

The key to maintaining a clutter-free home is consistency. Commit to these habits daily, even when life gets busy. Remember, it's better to spend a few minutes each day tidying than to face hours of cleaning later.

How to Stay Motivated:

- Set reminders or alarms to keep yourself on track.
- Reflect on how maintaining a clutter-free space enhances your well-being and productivity.

Monthly Check-ins: Reviewing and Fine-Tuning Your Systems

Maintaining a clutter-free lifestyle requires more than just an initial burst of organization; it's a continuous process of evaluation and adjustment. Monthly check-ins are an essential part of this process, offering you the opportunity to assess what's working, identify what isn't, and refine your systems to better suit your needs.

These regular reviews aren't about starting from scratch every month—they're about staying aligned with your goals and making incremental improvements. With consistent monthly check-ins, you'll ensure your home, workspace, and mindset remain clutter-free and functional.

1. Set Aside Time for Reflection

Dedicate a specific day or time each month for your check-in. Treat it like an appointment with yourself, blocking it off on your calendar to ensure it becomes a non-negotiable habit.

Why It Matters: Life gets busy, and without a designated time to reflect, it's easy for clutter to creep back in unnoticed. Monthly check-ins keep you proactive rather than reactive.

2. Evaluate Your Physical Space

Begin your check-in by walking through your home or workspace and observing your surroundings. Take note of areas that feel cluttered, disorganized, or inefficient.

Key Questions to Ask Yourself:

- Are there any "hotspots" where clutter tends to accumulate?
- Are your storage solutions working effectively?
- Is there anything you haven't used in the past month that could be removed or donated?

Action Step: Focus on decluttering one high-impact area during each monthly check-in. For example, if your kitchen counters have become a catch-all, dedicate 20–30 minutes to clearing and organizing them.

3. Review Your Systems

Your organizational systems should make life easier, not harder. Take a moment to evaluate whether your current systems are still serving you well.

Examples of Systems to Review:

- Filing systems for paperwork or digital files.
- Storage solutions for frequently used items.
- Routines for managing laundry, dishes, or other household tasks.

Why It's Important: As your needs and lifestyle change, your systems may need to adapt. A monthly review ensures they remain effective and relevant.

4. Check Your Calendar

A clutter-free life isn't just about physical spaces—it's also about managing your time and commitments. During your check-in, review your calendar to assess whether your schedule aligns with your priorities.

Questions to Consider:

- Are you overcommitted?
- Are there any activities or obligations you can let go of to create more space in your life?
- Are you dedicating time to the things that truly matter to you?

Action Step: Streamline your calendar by eliminating unnecessary commitments and scheduling downtime for yourself.

5. Reflect on Your Habits

Take stock of the daily and weekly habits you've been practicing to maintain a clutter-free lifestyle. Identify which habits are working well and which ones need reinforcement.

Helpful Questions:

- Am I sticking to my daily decluttering routines?
- Have I been following the "one in, one out" rule?
- Are there any habits I need to refine or recommit to?

Tip: If you've fallen off track with a particular habit, don't be too hard on yourself. Use this check-in as an opportunity to reset and refocus.

6. Declutter Emotionally and Mentally

Clutter isn't just physical; it can also manifest in your thoughts and emotions. Use your monthly check-in to reflect on your mental and emotional well-being.

Reflection Prompts:

- Are there any unresolved stresses or worries weighing me down?
- Do I feel overwhelmed or at peace with my current environment?
- What can I let go of—physically or emotionally—to feel lighter and more focused?

Why It's Crucial: Mental clarity and emotional well-being are foundational to sustaining a clutter-free lifestyle. Decluttering your mind helps you stay motivated and intentional.

7. Celebrate Progress

Take time to acknowledge and celebrate the progress you've made since your last check-in. Whether it's a cleaner closet, a more organized workspace, or simply feeling less stressed, every step forward is worth recognizing.

How to Celebrate:

- Reward yourself with a small treat, such as a relaxing evening or a new book.
- Reflect on how these changes have positively impacted your life.
- Share your progress with a friend or loved one for added motivation.

Why It Matters: Celebrating progress reinforces positive habits and keeps you motivated to continue your efforts.

Adopting a "Less Is More" Philosophy: Reinforcing Mindset Shifts for Long-Term Success

A clutter-free life isn't just about decluttering your space—it's about transforming your mindset. Adopting a "less is more" philosophy helps you focus on what truly matters, both in your physical environment and your overall lifestyle.

This mindset shift emphasizes quality over quantity, intentional living, and finding contentment with less. It's a powerful way to break free from the cycle of excess and create a life that feels lighter, simpler, and more meaningful.

1. Revaluate Your Relationship with "Stuff"

Many of us have been conditioned to equate happiness with material possessions. Adopting a "less is more" philosophy requires challenging this belief and redefining your relationship with "stuff."

Reflection Questions:

- Do the items I own truly bring me joy or serve a purpose?
- Am I holding onto things out of guilt, obligation, or fear?
- How would I feel if I had fewer possessions but more space and clarity?

Action Step: Practice gratitude for what you already have and focus on the value, not the volume, of your belongings.

2. Prioritize Quality Over Quantity

A "less is more" mindset prioritizes investing in high-quality items that last, rather than accumulating cheap, disposable goods. This approach applies to everything from clothing to kitchenware to furniture.

Why It's Effective: Fewer, better-quality items reduce clutter and create a sense of intentionality in your space.

Tip: When making a purchase, ask yourself, "Will this add long-term value to my life?"

3. Embrace Minimalism in Your Schedule

A clutter-free mindset extends beyond your possessions to how you spend your time. Overcommitting can lead to mental and emotional clutter, leaving you feeling overwhelmed and drained.

How to Simplify Your Schedule?

- Say no to activities or obligations that don't align with your values.
- Prioritize downtime and self-care.
- Focus on deep, meaningful connections rather than spreading yourself too thin.

Why It Matters: A simplified schedule allows you to be more present and intentional in your daily life.

4. Practice Mindful Consumption

Mindful consumption is at the heart of the "less is more" philosophy. It involves being deliberate about what you bring into your life and why.

Practical Tips:

- Avoid impulse purchases by waiting 24–48 hours before buying non-essential items.
- Focus on experiences and relationships rather than material possessions.
- Regularly assess your needs versus wants.

Why It's Powerful: Mindful consumption reduces waste, saves money, and helps you maintain a clutter-free environment.

5. Let Go of Perfectionism

A "less is more" mindset isn't about creating a picture-perfect home or lifestyle. It's about finding balance, embracing imperfection, and focusing on what truly matters.

How to Shift Your Mindset?

- Accept that some areas of your home or life will always be a work in progress.
- Focus on progress over perfection.
- Celebrate small victories and milestones.

Why It's Important: Letting go of perfectionism frees you from unnecessary stress and allows you to enjoy the process of simplifying your life.

6. Cultivate Gratitude

Gratitude is a cornerstone of the "less is more" philosophy. By focusing on what you have rather than what you lack, you shift your perspective and find contentment with less.

Daily Gratitude Practice:

- Write down three things you're grateful for each day.
- Reflect on the non-material aspects of your life that bring you joy and fulfilment.

Why It Works: Gratitude fosters a sense of abundance and reduces the desire for more "stuff."

7. Focus on Experiences, Not Possessions

Research shows that experiences bring more lasting happiness than material possessions. Adopting a "less is more" philosophy means prioritizing experiences—like spending time with loved ones, traveling, or pursuing hobbies—over accumulating things.

Action Step: Shift your spending habits to reflect this priority. For example, invest in a memorable family outing rather than buying more decorations for your home.

8. Inspire Others to Join You

A "less is more" mindset can be contagious. Share your journey with friends and family, and encourage them to embrace a simpler, more intentional lifestyle.

Ways to Inspire Others:

- Share your successes and lessons learned.
- Lead by example, demonstrating the benefits of a clutter-free life.
- Host a decluttering or donation event to encourage collective action.

Monthly check-ins and adopting a "less is more" philosophy are two powerful strategies for maintaining a clutter-free life and fostering long-term success. Together, they create a system of accountability, reflection, and intentionality that helps you stay on track and align your actions with your values.

By regularly reviewing your systems, celebrating progress, and embracing a mindset of simplicity, you'll not only keep clutter at bay but also create a life that feels lighter, freer, and more fulfilling. In this way, decluttering becomes more than just a task—it becomes a way of life.

Chapter 10: Embracing the Benefits of Decluttering

Stress Reduction: Transforming Your Spaces into Peaceful Sanctuaries

Stress has become an all-too-common companion. The environments we inhabit—whether at home, work, or elsewhere—play a significant role in influencing our mental and emotional well-being. Cluttered, chaotic spaces can heighten stress levels, while thoughtfully designed, serene environments can foster calm and relaxation. Transforming your spaces into peaceful sanctuaries isn't just about aesthetics; it's about creating environments that nurture your mind, body, and soul.

The Connection Between Space and Stress

1. The Psychological Impact of Clutter

Research shows that cluttered environments can overstimulate our senses, leading to feelings of overwhelm and anxiety. Clutter demands our attention, whether consciously or subconsciously, creating a constant sense of unfinished tasks.

- Mental Fatigue: Cluttered spaces make it difficult to focus, draining mental energy.
- Heightened Anxiety: A chaotic environment can mirror and amplify internal stress.
- Procrastination: The sheer volume of disorganized items can lead to decision fatigue, causing delays in taking action.

2. The Role of Calm Spaces in Stress Reduction

Conversely, organized and serene spaces encourage relaxation and mental clarity. A peaceful environment can:

- Lower cortisol levels, the hormone associated with stress.
- Improve focus and productivity.
- Create a sense of control and balance in daily life.

Steps to Transform Your Spaces into Peaceful Sanctuaries

1. Decluttering for Serenity

Decluttering is the foundation of a stress-free environment. Begin by assessing your space and identifying items that no longer serve a purpose or bring joy.

- Room-by-Room Approach: Tackle one area at a time to avoid overwhelm.
- The "Keep, Donate, Discard" Method: Sort items into these three categories to streamline decisions.
- Focus on Sentimental Items Last: Start with less emotionally charged areas to build momentum.

A decluttered space not only looks more inviting but also reduces the mental burden of visual chaos.

2. Incorporating Soothing Colours

Colours have a profound impact on our mood and emotions. When designing a stress-free sanctuary, prioritize calming hues.

- Neutral Tones: Shades like beige, taupe, and cream evoke warmth and tranquillity.

- Cool Colours: Soft blues, greens, and grays are known to reduce stress and promote relaxation.
- Avoid Overly Bright Colours: Vibrant reds or yellows can overstimulate and disrupt calmness.

3. Emphasizing Natural Light

Natural light has been shown to boost mood and reduce stress. Transform your space by maximizing access to sunlight.

- Open Curtains and Blinds: Let natural light flood your room during the day.
- Strategic Mirrors: Place mirrors to reflect and amplify light in darker areas.
- Use Sheer Curtains: Allow light to filter through while maintaining privacy.

For rooms with limited natural light, consider warm-toned artificial lighting that mimics sunlight.

4. Adding Elements of Nature

Basophilic design, which incorporates natural elements into indoor spaces, has been proven to reduce stress and enhance well-being.

- Houseplants: Greenery not only purifies the air but also creates a sense of vitality and calm.
- Natural Materials: Incorporate wood, stone, or bamboo for a grounded, earthy feel.
- Water Features: The soothing sound of a small fountain or aquarium can create a meditative atmosphere.

5. Creating Functional Zones

Disorganized spaces often blur the boundaries between activities, leading to confusion and stress. Designate specific zones for different functions.

- Work Zone: Keep your workspace free from distractions with organized supplies and minimal décor.
- Relaxation Zone: Dedicate an area to unwinding, complete with comfortable seating, soft lighting, and a cosy blanket.
- Sleep Zone: Ensure your bedroom is clutter-free, with soft bedding and a calming ambiance.

6. Sounds aping for Serenity

The sounds around us significantly influence our stress levels. Create a calming auditory environment by:

- Playing soft instrumental or nature-inspired music.
- Using white noise machines to drown out distractions.
- Incorporating sound-absorbing materials like rugs, curtains, or acoustic panels to reduce echoes.

Practical Tips for Maintaining Peaceful Spaces

1. Establish Daily Routines

Consistency is key to maintaining a stress-free environment. Simple habits can prevent clutter from accumulating:

- Morning Reset: Spend five minutes tidying up each morning.
- End-of-Day Ritual: Put away items and prepare your space for the next day.
- One-In-One-Out Rule: For every new item you bring in, remove one to maintain balance.

2. Embrace Minimalism

Adopting a minimalist approach can help reduce stress by limiting excess and focusing on essentials. Consider:

- Opting for quality over quantity in décor and furnishings.
- Keeping surfaces clear to create a sense of openness.
- Being intentional about new purchases to avoid unnecessary accumulation.

3. Personalizing Your Sanctuary

While a clean and organized space is essential, it's also important to make it feel like "home." Add personal touches that bring comfort and joy:

- Family photos or cherished mementos.
- A favourite scented candle or essential oil diffuser.
- Artwork or books that inspire and uplift.

4. Regular Check-Ins

Evaluate your spaces periodically to ensure they continue to meet your needs.

- Assess whether items are still serving their purpose.
- Reorganize areas that feel chaotic or overfilled.

- Refresh the space with small updates, such as new cushions or rearranged furniture.

The Emotional and Physical Benefits of Peaceful Spaces

Transforming your spaces into sanctuaries offers far-reaching benefits beyond reducing stress:

1. Enhanced Mental Clarity

An organized environment allows your mind to focus on what truly matters, improving decision-making and creativity.

2. Better Physical Health

Stress reduction through peaceful spaces can lead to improved sleep, lower blood pressure, and enhanced immune function.

3. Strengthened Relationships

A serene home fosters harmony among family members by reducing tension and encouraging positive interactions.

4. Increased Productivity

Functional, clutter-free zones help you stay focused and accomplish tasks more efficiently, whether at work or home.

5. Greater Sense of Control

Designing and maintaining peaceful spaces gives you a sense of empowerment and control over your environment.

Boosting Productivity

Productivity isn't just about doing more; it's about doing the right things effectively. By optimizing your focus, managing your energy, and eliminating distractions, you can maximize your output while minimizing stress.

1. The Science of Focus and Efficiency

To boost productivity, it's essential to understand the factors that influence focus and efficiency.

- Cognitive Load: Your brain can only handle a limited amount of information at once. Reducing unnecessary mental clutter—such as by decluttering your physical and digital environments—frees up cognitive resources for essential tasks.

- The Role of Breaks: Contrary to the myth of endless work, regular breaks enhance productivity by preventing burnout and improving concentration. Techniques like the Pomodoro Method emphasize short, focused work sessions followed by breaks.
- Energy Cycles: Recognize your peak productivity hours, whether you're a morning person or a night owl, and schedule high-priority tasks during these times.

2. Strategies for Enhanced Focus

Enhancing focus requires a combination of environmental adjustments, mental techniques, and consistent habits.

Minimize Distractions:

- Silence notifications on devices.
- Create a dedicated workspace free from clutter and interruptions.
- Use apps like Focus@Will or Forest to stay on track.

Practice Single-Tasking:

- Multitasking dilutes focus and reduces efficiency. Prioritize one task at a time to achieve deeper engagement and better results.

Adopt Time-Blocking:

- Allocate specific blocks of time for different activities. This structured approach ensures that essential tasks receive dedicated attention.

Set SMART Goals:

- Break down objectives into Specific, Measurable, Achievable, Relevant, and Time-bound steps. Clear goals provide direction and reduce decision fatigue.

3. Systems and Tools for Productivity

Harnessing tools and systems can streamline workflows and improve organization.

- Task Management Apps: Platforms like Todoist, Trello, or Asana help you track tasks, set priorities, and collaborate with others.

- Digital Calendars: Tools like Google Calendar or Microsoft Outlook allow you to schedule tasks, set reminders, and avoid overbooking your time.
- Automation: Automate repetitive tasks using tools like Zapier or IFTTT to save time and energy.

4. The Role of Decluttering in Productivity

Physical and digital clutter creates unnecessary distractions, sapping focus and energy. Decluttering your environment can significantly enhance productivity.

- Organize Your Workspace: Keep only essential items on your desk, and use storage solutions to maintain order.
- Streamline Digital Files: Use folder systems and cloud storage to manage documents, and regularly clear your email inbox.
- Adopt Minimalist Practices: Simplify your belongings and commitments to focus on what truly adds value.

5. The Power of Routines and Habits

Consistent routines provide structure, reduce decision fatigue, and create momentum.

- Morning Routines: Start your day with energizing habits, such as exercise, meditation, or journaling, to set a positive tone.
- Evening Routines: Wind down with activities like reading, planning the next day, or practicing gratitude to ensure restful sleep.
- Keystone Habits: Focus on transformative habits, such as regular exercise or meal planning, which positively impact other areas of your life.

Living with Intention

Living with intention means aligning your time, energy, and actions with your core values and long-term goals. This approach fosters a sense of purpose, satisfaction, and fulfilment.

1. Defining Your Intentions

The first step to living intentionally is clarifying what truly matters to you.

- Reflect on Your Values: Consider what principles and ideals guide your decisions, such as family, health, creativity, or community.

- Set Long-Term Goals: Identify aspirations that resonate with your values, whether they involve personal growth, relationships, or career achievements.
- Prioritize What Matters Most: Evaluate your current commitments and focus on those that align with your intentions.

2. Cultivating Mindful Awareness

Mindfulness is a powerful tool for intentional living. By staying present in the moment, you can make conscious choices and appreciate the journey.

- Practice Gratitude: Regularly acknowledge the positives in your life to cultivate a sense of contentment.
- Engage Fully: Give your undivided attention to the task or person at hand, avoiding the distractions of multitasking or overthinking.
- Embrace Simplicity: Focus on what truly adds value, letting go of excess or unnecessary pursuits.

3. Redirecting Time and Energy

Living with intention often requires re-examining how you allocate your resources.

- Conduct a Time Audit: Track how you spend your time for a week to identify areas of inefficiency or misalignment with your goals.
- Say No Strategically: Learn to decline commitments that don't align with your values, freeing up time for what matters most.
- Focus on Quality Over Quantity: Prioritize deep, meaningful experiences over superficial or fleeting ones.

4. Building Resilience Through Purpose

A strong sense of purpose can help you navigate challenges and stay committed to your intentions.

- Find Meaning in Your Work: Look for ways to connect your daily tasks to larger goals or values.
- Celebrate Progress: Acknowledge milestones and successes, no matter how small, to maintain motivation.
- Stay Flexible: Life is unpredictable, and living intentionally doesn't mean rigidly adhering to a

plan. Adapt as needed while staying true to your core values.

5. The Role of Community and Relationships

Intentional living thrives in the context of supportive relationships and communities.

- Surround Yourself with Like-Minded People: Seek out individuals who share your values and aspirations.
- Invest in Relationships: Prioritize meaningful connections by spending quality time with loved ones.
- Contribute to Your Community: Volunteer or engage in activities that align with your intentions, fostering a sense of purpose and belonging.

Integrating Productivity and Intentional Living

Productivity and intentional living are not mutually exclusive; they complement and reinforce each other. By enhancing focus and efficiency, you free up time and energy to invest in what truly matters. Conversely, living intentionally ensures your efforts are directed toward meaningful pursuits, maximizing the impact of your productivity.

- Create Alignment: Regularly review your goals and adjust your efforts to ensure they reflect your values.
- Embrace the Journey: Recognize that both productivity and intentional living are ongoing processes, requiring reflection, adjustment, and growth.
- Balance Action and Reflection: Dedicate time to both achieving results and contemplating your direction.

Decluttering Challenges: 30-Day Plans and Checklists

Week 1: Preparing and Starting Small

Day 1:

Identify your clutter hotspots and set a goal. Take a walk around your space and make a list of the areas that feel overwhelming or stressful. Set a specific and realistic goal for what you want to achieve by the end of the decluttering process.

Day 2:

Clear one small space (e.g., a single drawer). Choose a small, manageable area to begin with, like a drawer you use daily. Empty it completely, sort items into categories (keep, donate, or trash), and return only what is essential or brings you joy.

Day 3:

Begin a "One-In-One-Out" rule for new items. For every new item you bring into your space, commit to removing one item. This habit prevents new clutter from building up and helps you maintain balance in your belongings.

Day 4:

Tackle paper clutter (e.g., old bills, receipts). Sort through piles of paper and categorize them into keep, shred, or recycle. Use folders or digital tools to organize important documents and reduce future paper clutter.

Day 5:

Declutter your purse, bag, or wallet. Empty everything out and sort the contents into categories: essentials, trash, and items to relocate. Only return items that you use daily or truly need, and establish a routine for keeping your bag organized.

Day 6:

Create a donation box and add at least five items. Find items you no longer need or use but are still in good condition. Place them in a designated box for donation and commit to dropping them off at a local charity or thrift store.

Day 7:

Reflect on progress and adjust your strategy. Take time to review what you've accomplished so far and identify any areas where you faced challenges. Use this reflection to refine your decluttering approach and set realistic goals for the coming weeks.

Week 2: Decluttering Key Areas

Day 8:

Focus on your kitchen counters and pantry. Clear your kitchen counters of non-essential items to create an open, functional workspace. Then, organize your pantry by grouping similar items, discarding expired goods, and using clear containers or labels for easy access.

Day 9:

Organize a single closet or wardrobe section. Choose one section of your closet, such as a shelf or hanging rod. Remove everything, sort items into categories (keep, donate, discard), and neatly return only what you love and use regularly. Use organizers for smaller items.

Day 10:

Eliminate digital clutter (e.g., unused apps, old files). Review your devices and remove apps you no longer use, delete unnecessary files, and organize important documents into clearly labelled folders. Consider using cloud storage for better accessibility and backups.

Day 11:

Declutter your bathroom shelves and drawers. Remove all items from shelves and drawers, discard expired products, and group similar items together. Clean the surfaces before returning only the essentials, and use organizers for better functionality.

Day 12:

Sort through sentimental items (limit to 15 minutes). Set a timer and focus on a small batch of sentimental items, like photos or keepsakes. Decide what truly holds value and let go of items that no longer bring joy or serve a purpose, keeping only the most meaningful pieces.

Day 13:

Optimize your workspace (desk and surrounding area). Clear your desk and surrounding area of unnecessary items, organize your essentials for easy access, and create a layout that enhances focus and productivity. Consider adding personal touches like a plant or motivational quote to make it inviting.

Day 14:

Take a day to enjoy your decluttered spaces. Use this time to relax and appreciate the transformation you've achieved so far. Reflect on how these changes make your space feel more functional and peaceful, reinforcing the benefits of maintaining a clutter-free lifestyle.

Week 3: Deep Dive into Problem Areas

Day 15:

Tackle one "dumping ground" area (e.g., junk drawer). Identify a space that tends to collect random items, like a junk drawer or countertop. Empty it completely, sort through the contents, and only return items that belong there. Find proper homes for everything else.

Day 16:

Go through books and media (keep favourites only). Review your collection of books, DVDs, and other media. Keep the items that you truly enjoy or revisit regularly. Donate or recycle those that no longer align with your interests or bring you joy.

Day 17:

Sort seasonal or holiday decorations. Review your collection of seasonal items, discarding anything broken or unused. Group similar decorations together, label storage containers clearly, and store them in an accessible yet out-of-the-way location for ease of use next season.

Day 18:

Declutter kids' toys or shared family spaces. Focus on areas used by the whole family or children, such as playrooms or common rooms. Sort toys and items into categories, involve kids in deciding what to keep, and create a system for organizing shared spaces to maintain order.

Day 19:

Organize cords, chargers, and electronic gadgets. Gather all your electronic items, untangle cords, and test gadgets to ensure they work. Use cord organizers or labelled bags to store cables neatly and designate a specific drawer or box for gadgets and accessories.

Day 20:

Focus on shoes and accessories. Sort through your shoes and accessories, such as belts, scarves, and jewellery. Discard items that are worn out or no longer match your style. Organize the remaining pieces using storage solutions like shoe racks, hooks, or small boxes for easy access and visibility.

Day 21:

Reassess areas already decluttered for stray items. Take a moment to revisit previously decluttered spaces to ensure they remain tidy. Look for items that may have wandered back and return them to their proper places or decide if they are no longer needed.

Week 4: Maintenance and Long-Term Habits

Day 22:

Create a system for incoming mail and papers. Designate a specific spot for incoming mail and papers, such as a tray or folder. Sort items daily into categories like urgent, to file, and to discard. This habit prevents pileups and keeps important documents easily accessible.

Day 23:

Establish a weekly decluttering schedule. Choose a dedicated day each week to tidy up and address areas where clutter tends to accumulate. Regular maintenance prevents clutter from building up again and helps you stay on top of your newly organized spaces.

Day 24:

Donate or dispose of items from your "to-go" boxes. Take the time to follow through on your decluttering efforts by delivering donation items to a local charity or arranging for a pickup. Properly dispose of broken or unusable items to free up space and ensure nothing lingers unnecessarily.

Day 25:

Set rules for future purchases (e.g., quality over quantity). Establish guidelines to prevent future clutter, such as prioritizing durable, high-quality items over cheap, disposable ones. Consider implementing a waiting period before buying non-essential items to ensure thoughtful, intentional purchasing decisions.

Day 26:

Simplify your digital life (e.g., unsubscribe from emails). Spend time reviewing your digital clutter by unsubscribing from unnecessary email lists, deleting unused apps, and organizing your files into labelled folders. This helps reduce digital noise and improves focus and efficiency in your daily life.

Day 27:

Plan a clutter-free habit for each family member. Encourage each family member to adopt a simple habit that contributes to a clutter-free home, such as putting away their belongings daily or decluttering their personal space weekly. These small, consistent actions foster shared responsibility and long-term success.

Day 28:

Do a final review of all decluttered areas? Walk through each space you've worked on and check for any remaining clutter or areas that need adjustment. Take note of what systems are working well and identify areas that might need further improvement. This step solidifies your progress and ensures a smooth transition to maintenance.

Day 29:

Celebrate your progress and reflect on your journey. Take a moment to acknowledge how far you've come and the positive changes you've made. Reflect on the challenges you overcame, the lessons learned, and how these efforts have improved your environment and well-being. Reward yourself for your hard work with something meaningful, such as a relaxing day or a small treat.

Day 30:

Create a vision board for maintaining a clutter-free life. Use images, words, and symbols that represent your ideal clutter-free environment. Place this board where you can see it daily as a visual reminder of your goals and the benefits of decluttering.

Printed in Great Britain
by Amazon

da26819d-2869-4148-8dac-40e4ef3358f6R01